How to Overcome Depression as a Christian

A Biblical and Scientific Perspective for People Who Totally Lost Their Hope and Believe There Is Nothing Left

Andrei Nedelcu

BONUS!

I'm glad and I want to thank you for buying my book. I sincerely hope it will be of great use to you. As a thank you, I am happy to give you a small gift. Also, if you want more resources in the field of psychology, I will be honored to help you. Thank you and take care! Simple follow the link for **FREE ACCESS!**

10 Biblical Principles For a Healthy Mind

Enter the following link in the browser:

https://bit.ly/30bHRVr

INTRODUCTION								6

CHAPTER 1. THE TRAP								9

CHAPTER 2. THE BIBLE AND DEPRESSION								15

CHAPTER 3. WHAT IS DEPRESSION?								27

CHAPTER 4. THE CAUSES OF DEPRESSION								35

PART TWO.								45

CHAPTER 5. TREATMENT OF DEPRESSION								46

CHAPTER 6. BEHAVIORAL ACTIVATION								50

CHAPTER 7. POSITIVE EMOTION								57

CHAPTER 8. MAXIMIZING SLEEP QUALITY								64

CHAPTER 9. WINNING THE BATTLE WITH BAD THOUGHTS								71

CHAPTER 10. PHYSICAL ACTIVITY								85

CHAPTER 11. WHERE IS GOD WHEN WE SUFFER								91

CONCLUSION								95

BIBLIOGRAPHY								96

Introduction

You may think you do not deserve in any way, what has happened to you so far, all the trials and tribulations alike. You may be convinced that what is happening to you now is not right either. Maybe *you have reached the point* where few things give you meaning and satisfaction or any prayer you offer seems to stop with a lot of enthusiasm on the ceiling, without getting the expected answer.

The main reason I wrote this book is for the Christian who has reached the end of his powers, for one reason or another.

The truth is that each of us, no matter how strong, has **an end of powers**, a finite limit that once reached, makes impossible any kind of advancement and progress our mind could paint.

This **end of the powers** does not necessarily mean we no longer have faith in God. It is possible that trust in Him will remain intact, but trust in us will be shaken from all foundations. The end of the powers does not mean we refuse to get up and move on, being cowards who want to escape from reality. But it means we do not know how we could get up, we do not find the slightest trace of power and we sink, deeper and deeper, with every minute, hour and day that flows from our lives.

When we reach such times in our lives and I am convinced that we will, we need to recalculate things and accept any helping hand that is offered to us, both from God and from the people He has given to us, sitting next to us.

The reader may conclude he has never been in such a position and rightly so. Some have been predestined to be brave and strong all their lives or maybe not. However, what about the one next to us who has reached the end of their powers? How do we intend to be next to the one who sees no shade except black and who is willing to give up the battle of life at any time, putting down his weapons? Or what about the one who lives but does not enjoy any moment of his "miserable existence?"

There is a possibility that these truths will help him regain his strength, if we take our role seriously, having the knowledge and willingness to help him.

In this paper, you will find theoretical and practical knowledge about how the human mind works, when it reaches the end of its powers, paralyzed by the troubles and inconveniences of everyday life.

Jesus predicted and warned us in the pages of the Bible that we would go through such times: *"I have told you these things, that in me you may have peace. In the world you have oppression; but cheer up! I have overcome the world."* John 16:33.

With God's help in the contents of this book you will find ways to dare. And boldness is not an option, but a commandment of great significance, said by the One who created the human mind, daring the former.

The secondary reason I struggled to write these things is related to the perspective that many of us who know God have.

It is possible that some of us have fallen into the deep trap of saying that a man of God *"should never reach the end of his powers."* A man who has a relationship with God "should never" be depressed under any circumstances. We will return to the implications of this issue later. However, the Holy

7

Scriptures and the reality of life, conceptualize things in a different way, and this we will continue to explore with special attention.

So, we set out to walk together in the way that helps us bring the truth to light, because only the truth has the consequence of freeing us (John 8:32).

My intention is for these thoughts to be suitable for both: erudite minds and those that function in a simpler and more practical register.

At the same time, this knowledge is intended for both those who are going through a period of crisis and those who want to guard their minds and improve certain aspects of their minds. A wise saying in folklore says that no matter how good it is, there is always a place for something better.

I will address the issue of depression and hopelessness from two broad perspectives. First, we will learn to identify it in the Bible, via God's people who have become hopeless at the end of their power.

At the same time, we will look at things through the lens of science, that will help us understand to some extent the causes of depression and loss of meaning, its symptoms and how our mind works. And finally, we will learn what are the ways in which we can dare and fight the good fight of faith (1 Timothy 6:12), integrating what Scripture tells us, with what science tells us.

CHAPTER 1. The Trap

"A true Christian should never have depression."

Across the Earth, every year, about 7% (264 million) of people of all ages, report suffering from this terrible disorder called depression. Among the people who suffer from this disease, about 800,000 (almost one million people) decide every year that life has no meaning and is not worth living.

At the time of writing, there are 161,283 people who have died from the "cause" of the COVID-19 virus and so much hustle and bustle has been created in our minds. But did you know that almost 1,000,000 people give up their lives every year? And yet we still have no reaction and often joke about all this "propaganda" with depression, trying to convince ourselves of our own strength and the fact that only the weak can give up the end of power.

What is even more worrying is that suicide is the second leading cause of death for people aged 15-29. Young people suffer in silence.

The main people who are more vulnerable to giving up on life are those who struggle with various mental problems, the most notable of which are depression and alcohol consumption. [1]

Available statistics show that in the USA (United States of America), about 123 people give up on their daily lives, the average reaching 44,965 people each year. One thing worth mentioning is that only half of people who suffer from depression end up receiving treatment. For every 25 suicide attempts, there is a successful one and every 40 seconds, someone dies because of suicide. [2]

Christianity and depression

A study conducted in 2009 showed there are no significant differences between the frequency of depression in religious groups (those who go to religious services) compared to those who are not religious and do not participate in such services. [3]

In one of the relevant studies on this topic, 1,000 Protestant pastors were included and the following results were reported: about 3 out of 4 pastors said they knew someone in their family, friends or church who had been diagnosed with bipolar disorder, 74% said they know someone diagnosed with major depression, and 57% said they know at least 3 people who have had clinical depression.

Very interesting is the fact that most pastors have reported that there is very little training to recognize mental problems. Extremely few churches have a plan to help families in which someone has been diagnosed with a mental illness. The churches that do not have a counselor ready to intervene on these mental issues are in the same tonality. [4]

The deep Trap "A Christian should not fight with depression"

According to what evidence and reasoning do we accept so easily this erroneous belief? Is there an accredited document that validates this wrong conclusion?

There is a lack of knowledge that prevents our eyes from seeing reality as it is (Hosea 4:6). A mental disorder such as depression is no different from a physical illness. Our brains are the most important and fascinating organs, and they can get sick, just like the heart, kidneys, lungs or liver.

The truth is that nowhere in the Holy Scriptures has God promised us full immunity from the arrows of depression or mental problems. There is no biblical verse on the basis of which we can say that a true Christian will not end up struggling with depression or other such problems. On the contrary, there are people on the pages of the Bible who have struggled with depression and reached the very end of their power, as we will see in the next chapter.

Why is this belief a terrible trap in itself? Not only is it unfounded in God's Word, but it also causes a great deal of damage. Suppose, for the sake of argument, that this false and unrealistic belief is true. If a Christian struggle with depression, his mind will deduce that what is happening to him is due to the fact he does not have enough faith, because he is too weak.

This bad and sneaking thought will cause him a lot of pain, shame and guilt, an aspect that will dramatically accentuate the symptoms of depression and hopelessness. "*I shouldn't be depressed, but still, I am guilty of lack of faith and everything that happens to me.*" Moreover, accepting such an irrational thought would prevent the Christian from asking for help and admitting he is sinking, feeling terribly guilty and ashamed of what is happening to him.

Should Peter have sunk when he tried to go to sea? Obviously not, but he still sank and instantly acknowledged this was happening. If he had thought in this pattern, "*I should not sink,*" he certainly would not have asked for the Lord Jesus to save him.

The accident that "shouldn't" happen

Let me use a short image to clarify the issue. Imagine witnessing an accident involving dramatic consequences. Instead of accepting the accident happened and that there are victims who are suffering, you turn your head in the opposite direction and say the following: *"This accident should not happen. It happened because the driver didn't pay enough attention."* Do you notice the irrationality here?

Whatever is the cause of the accedent and the pain, it is there, happening, and requires care, empathy, and involvement. Who made us decide what should happen and what should not happen? Yes, it would have been ideal for the accident not to have taken place, but unfortunately it did happen and there are two alternatives. We recognize it is happening and we lend a helping hand or we pretend nothing is happening and we go with a lot of fullness in the opposite direction.

Misery hidden in an artistic way

Each of us has seen or can form the image of a carpet in our minds. The human mind has an incredible ability to introduce misery into it. Think that under the rug of life, disorder of all kinds can be introduced: negative emotions, stress at work, a busy schedule and activities that hardly bring us fulfillment, a problem we failed to get over, such as the loss of a loved one, a breakup that totally destabilized our life plans, failure after failure, bitterness, resentment, disappointment, etc.

None of us live without breaking God's rules and without accumulating, in one way or another, a certain kind of filth under the rug. *"A Christian should not be miserable under the rug of his life."* is an unapproved and malicious conviction.

It is this conviction that prevents us from setting aside the carpet, cleansing what is to be cleansed, and living a full life, with the Lord and with our loved ones.

If we continue in the same way we can say that a Christian should not sin, yet does not the reverse happen many times? Then there is a need for acceptance of reality, repentance and correction that will bring rehabilitation. That is why the Lord Jesus came to this Earth, because we could not do "what should have been. *Should we get cancer? Should we have diabetes? Should...*

No matter how much we want to hide the dirt under a certain carpet, at some point there will be no room, it will either come to the surface alone due to the discomfort, or it will start to "smell hard." [5] When we introduce impurities into our minds, it will leave its print and become part of who we are.

In closing this chapter, I encourage you not to throw stones at those who are at the end of their powers. Never allow ourselves to point the finger at someone who is suffering just because our mind is too limited to understand their suffering. It is not our mission to make them feel toxic shame and guilt that will push them to hide their problems or give up "fighting the good fight of faith."

It is not our mission to determine why they got there, before we lean towards their carpet and help them with sincerity, tears and dedication to make order there. The best thing you can do for someone you don't understand is to not confuse them even more. Don't look so brave, because you never know when God will decide to teach you a lesson and it's your turn. As C.S. Lewis says, he lives and lets others live.

For the person who does not understand the gravity of the situation and makes fun of it, *"I have to try my best to feel at least pity, there can be no question of sympathy."* [6]

For those who have reached the end of their powers, you are not alone. There are people of God who have in turn crossed the same dark path. Do not lose hope and do not give up on asking God to help you cleanse the carpet of your life (Romans 12: 2).

CHAPTER 2. The Bible and Depression

"A sad soul can kill you quicker, far quicker, than a germ."
Jon Steinbeck.

When we approach to read and study God's Word seriously, we will not find the word *depression* in most translations. This is one of the main reasons why some of us have become trapped in the trap described in the previous chapter. One of the few passages that more clearly emphasizes this problem is Proverbs 12:25, in which we find that anxiety in the human mind can bring him down.

However, we will find in the Bible similar words that define the same construct. Among these we can observe related concepts such as: troubled, saddened, desperate, hopeless, sad to death, mourning, and groaning. When we want to study different problems, in separate time periods, it is extremely important to understand that the same phenomenon was named and renamed according to how the problem was understood in that period.

What I am trying to highlight is the fact that depression has always existed, in different amounts of course and expressed in different ways, which is why we will study more closely the lives of some great people of God, who struggled with depression and they have had turbulence throughout their lives, sometimes even reaching the end of their powers.

1.The example of King David, a man after God's own heart

(Acts 13:22)

There is no more appropriate characterization than God makes to this man. God Himself described him as *"the man after the heart of God."* All who were contemporaries of King

David, knew a few important things about him: he knew how to play the harp extraordinarily, he was a strong and sturdy man, one of the greatest and bravest warriors, he spoke well, and he was goodly to look at. But the most the important thing was that God himself was with him (1 Samuel 16:18).

About half of the Psalms are composed by this great poet. We find this man mentioned in the Bible in over 900 verses. Fascinating, isn't it?

While all the people of Israel trembled with fear and were shaken with fear in the front of giant Goliath, a boy with ruddy hair, the son of Jesse, appears with an unshakable faith and offers to fight the Philistine giant himself. Who was David? A true warrior, a fearless titan who had a strong trust in God, which was hardened by the giants of his time. But beware, this is just one of the perspectives that David had. No man is in only one way. Let's turn our eyes to other facets of the same David, which we find detailed in Holy Scripture.

The first facet is found in (Psalm 143: 4,7) which we know is written by King David himself. Although the context is not specified, those who have studied the chronology of the Bible say that this writing dates back to the time when he counted the people of Israel.

"Therefore is my spirit overwhelmed within me, my heart within me is desolate, O Lord, my spirit faileth, hide not thy face from me."

It is about the same brave warrior, David, who shows symptoms of grief, of turmoil and who considers that God has turned away from him and left him. The Bible teaches that his mood often varies, and we can say without error that he was sometimes up, sometimes down.

16

Another reality was that the man of God faced was one of mourning, that he makes known to us in the songs he composed (Psalm 30:11). Interestingly, unlike many of us, the King of Israel does not try to hide the negative emotions he feels, nor does he pretend they do not exist.

Another perspective described in the Bible by David is that of a broken heart and a broken spirit. We can see in many of the Psalms written by the man of God that he had moments of defeat, sadness, mourning, loss of clarity and vision. Although we are dealing with a brave man, who had God in the battles of his life, there were situations in which this brave man, chosen by God, considered that God had forgotten him and that he was no longer present in his life.

One of the roles of the Psalms was to unload your soul before God. David had a troubled soul, much emotional distress, and a mind seized by the troubles of life, as he describes himself (Psalm 13: 1,2,3). Don't we really like to see the image of a such a David?

It's hard for us to imagine and accept such a hero, isn't it? However, it is the accurate, undistorted reality that we find revealed in the pages of Holy Scripture. David experienced despair, depression, sadness, pain, and experienced situations where he was down to earth without the clarity and resources to move on.

2.The gentlest man on Earth (Numbers 12:3)

The Old Testament introduces us to one of the people God loved the most. Moses is a highly educated person whom God convinces and uses to free the people of Israel from the harsh bondage of Egypt. We are told he had this fascinating feature:

he was the gentlest man on Earth. However, he was more than that. He was the only person among all the people to whom God revealed himself in a completely different way: face to face or mouth to mouth. When Moses was in the presence of God, he could see some of His glory and more than that, his eyes were given to see the image of God (Numbers 12: 8).

A whole book can be written about this man, who God has used, but I want to limit myself only to the fundamental aspects that contribute to the development of our subject. The responsibility that fell on Moses' shoulders was a huge one, and he was responsible for the direction in which the people of Israel were taking it.

There were many situations in which he struggled with the opposition and resistance of the people, various complaints and rejection even from those close to his heart (Numbers 12: 2).

In one of the classic rebellious contexts of the Jewish people, Moses gives in to pain and makes some statements that are difficult to digest. But they were not mere statements, they were thoughts of a reality he was struggling with.

"And if thou deal thus with me, kill me, I pray thee, out of hand, if I have found favor in thy sight, and let me not see my wretchedness," Numbers 11:15.

In another translation, his words are worded as follows: simply kill me, do me a favor, and save me from this misery. [7] We can identify from this passage the negative emotions that Moses felt: despair, disappointment, and hopelessness. Sometimes God's tasks may seem far, far too heavy to bear.

Even though God himself was with him, in this difficult context, primed by the problems created by those for whom he guaranteed, he no longer saw any way out. In those moments, he would have preferred to die rather than continue what he had to do. Let us not forget that Moses was a man with a great faith in God, and yet he went through many hard and unbearable times.

3. Elijah the prophet through whom fire descended from Heaven

We know about the prophet Elijah and that God chose him to speak against King Ahab and Queen Isabella because of their iniquities and uncleanness. God repeatedly took care of him and even sent certain birds to feed him. Through his hands great miracles were performed, such as the multiplication of oil or flour, in times when famine haunted the land of Israel. Moreover, we know about Elijah, that he resurrected the widow's son from Zarephath and was regarded as a man of God. In fact, there was no doubt that he would not be a man of God (1 Kings 17:24).

Another aspect Scripture tells us about this man is that God spoke to him (1 Kings 18: 1). In other words, he followed God's plan for him and had a strong, real connection with God. If we dig deeper, we will see that this prophet was not afraid of his profession. He had the courage to confront Ahab and tell him directly in front of him that he was the reason for the misfortune of the Jewish people and that it was because both he and his parents had deviated from God's laws.

Looking more closely we can see how Elijah provoked and confronted all the false prophets of those times. To have the courage to stand against 850 people, in front of the whole

19

nation, is not equivalent to fear, is it? Not only did he oppose them, but he also mocked them (1 Kings 18:27).

The altar of God, which had been broken by these false prophets of Baal, was rebuilt by him, who had the audacity to subject God to an absolutely admirable test. Because trusting in God the prophet asked for a sign that few people had the courage to ask for: fire from Heaven. His request was granted (1 Kings 18:37, 38). Thus through him, God showed His glory and proved to all people that He is the true God, the only true God, the Creator of all things. Later, Elijah killed all the false prophets, killed all the charlatans who led the people astray. What a man full of power and boldness, isn't he? We need such people even in these blurred times.

However, I forgot to mention another interesting episode about the same person. He had the courage to face an emperor, he had the courage to provoke 850 people in front of the whole Jewish nation, he had the audacity to kill them with the help of God and with the help of the people, but he got into big trouble in front of a woman as it is related to us in 1 Kings 19: 2, 3:

"Then Jezebel sent a messenger into Elijah, saying, so let the gods do tome, and more also, if i make not thy life as the life of one of them by tomorrow about this time."

From this story we can extract some basic ideas: indeed, Jezebel was not joking, she intended to kill and even managed to do so with great skill, so we can say she was a woman who had potential (1 Kings 18: 4). However, if you wanted to hurt someone or even take their life, would you send them notices to warn them? Obviously not. If you were serious, you would go straight to the register called facts.

Look at the consequences of a single threat to the mind of Elijah, a special man who had much power from God. The first symptom found is that of isolation. We see here an Elijah, depressed, fallen and tired of some words, who is alienated from everyone and runs away in the desert alone. Very interesting, isn't it?

If we had done a psychological examination today, we would most likely have diagnosed him with major depression, with an increased suicide risk, in principle it necessarily requires hospitalization and careful observation.

Not only did he isolate himself from the others, but being sad and abandoned there, he also started flirting with suicidal thoughts:

"But he himself went a day's journey into the wilderness, and came and sat down under a juniper tree: and he requested for himself that he might die, and said: It's enough, now, O LORD, take away my life; for I am not better than my fathers," 1 Kings 19:4.

It is difficult to look at such a man, with such power, with special reference, who has reached the end of his powers. Fortunately for him, God had mercy on Him and he directly benefited from the divine intervention that gave him the strength to move on and convinced him to continue his journey of life. But Elijah, no matter how strong, had moments of despair, and these are revealed to us in order to truly understand the magnitude of the problem. If you still think only weak and unbelieving people can fight depression, can it be said that they were all weak people? Are we stronger than them?

4. The condition of the sons of Korah (Psalm 42)

The sons of Korah describe very expressively, the state or mood they had for some time. In verse 3 we are told what food they ate day and night:

"My tears have been my meat day and night, while they continually say unto me, where is thy God?".

Paraphrasing what they said, they wept compulsively, day and night, because they no longer saw their God at work among them. Looking further, we notice a sadness raised to the highest standards. It was not a simple, insignificant sadness, but a heavy grief, an extremely intense pain, present in their being. I will +point out some important symptoms as they relate themselves:

" I remember, and I poured all the fire of my heart into me. Why do you grieve, souls, and groan within me? My soul is grieved within me, O God. One wave calls another wave, at the roar of the fall of Your waters; all thy waves and thy waves pass over me." (Psalm 42: 4, 5, 6,7).

Can you imagine the mood of these skilled singers? Desperate, saddened, full of unanswered questions and buried in the waves of trouble that can flood our minds. In this writing, there is more than just sadness. In fact, these singers were very convinced that God had forgotten them, that they had been forsaken, that He, the Creator of Heaven and Earth, was no longer there, leaving them to the enemy. This made them sad (Psalm 42: 9).

The pressure they experienced was real, overwhelming. Large enough to manifest not only in the mind but also in the body. We know today that this is called somatization, and we will

22

return to this issue in a later chapter. The suffering reported by them was imprinted in their very bones, in their whole being: *"As with a sword in my bones, mine enemies reproach me; while they say daily unto me, Where is thy God?"*

Usually when we are not heard, but we really want to be heard, we start very tactfully to raise the voice and if necessary to shout a little, eventually for capture attention.

These people try to make themselves heard, but not by shouting, but by repeating the same thing (42: 5, 11). We are shown the pain and sorrow of their souls, the emotions they felt, just so as not to conclude that we are always guarded by them. In other translations their position is signaled as follows: "Why are you desperate, my soul?" [8] Why are you thrown to the ground? They had constant crying day and night, memories that accentuated their sadness, a huge grief of the soul, moans, the prospect that God had forgotten them and a physical pain specific to the content of their minds.

Did Korah's sons have an accurate picture of God? Yes, they themselves urged their souls to trust in God and bring praise to Him. Did they know that God is their salvation? Of course, they asserted these truths without hesitation (Psalm 42: 5, 11). However, did the symptoms and troubles they had disappear? Does the pain and pressure of their soul change?

We learn from these examples, not to ignore the struggles of those in suffering. Let's not show a cynical attitude, let's keep up to date with their problems. Let's understand them and not burden them even more.

5. One of the heroes of childhood: The man eaten by fish

With the reader's kindness, I would like to give one last example. God gives a precise mission to Jonah, to go to Nineveh, a fornicating city, and to tell them that they will be destroyed if they do not rectify the situation. But instead of telling his enemies this life-saving news, he chooses to flee to the sea, far from God, and thus endangers the lives of the entire crew. God sends a storm to stop him from this rebellion and at his recommendations, his colleagues from the boat throw him into the sea, where he is swallowed by a huge fish.

For three days and three nights, Jonah had the opportunity to "come to his senses," apologizing, and apparently we assumed he had learned from his own past. In the end, he agrees to do what he had to do from the beginning. He goes to Nineveh, tells the people the sentence, and they return to God with repentance, regret, and a radical change of behavior.

We would expect Jonah to be satisfied, however, that a large fortress, with more than 120,000 people, was spared. Instead, his mood varies from anger to sadness, unspecific to the situation. Due to the fact that God's plan did not live up to his expectations, he asks God the same thing that the prophet Elijah asked for, death:

"Therefore now, O LORD, take, I beseech thee, my life from me, for it is better for me to die that to live." Jonah 4:3.

Scripture does not explicitly state whether Jonah was very depressed, but it does state that he left the city and isolated himself from everyone else for a simple reason. He was extremely angry. I saw earlier that Elijah was very depressed and had lost the trust he had gained with God throughout his experience.

This is not the case with Jonah, he experiences things a little differently. He was angry enough not to see the meaning of this life. I see black in front of my eyes, someone said. He was so angry that he was ready to give up, laying down his weapons.

Anger is another strong emotion that can darken our minds when we are at the end of our powers. We can get angry with God or others for a variety of reasons. The key aspect I want to emphasize here is that impulsivity can be so intense, so relentless, that it deprives us of the most valuable good: life.

Summarization

At the end of this chapter, I want you to keep some clear and well-marked conclusions in mind.

First of all, it is crucial to understand that I do not intend to make any diagnosis of God's people, far from me this thought. But I think the time has come to look at ourselves with all sincerity and to see that the Bible never hides the depressions and failures of its heroes. It is time to not hide our depressions and impurities anymore, it is time for the truth. The time has come to line up and stop blaming the suffering people. Today and now is the ideal time to put the bone to work.

The second important conclusion is that if God wants to use depression and despair with us and lead us to the end of our powers, he will. There is no biblical promise that God will not use emotional pain or allow us to be depressed, just to transform and renew certain aspects of our lives. He will do it according to the plan of His will, as He wills.

Thirdly, there are situations which by their nature imply a fall in proportions. There are contexts that by themselves, bring a lot of disappointment, pain, bitterness. It doesn't matter how strong we are. We can be disappointed in ourselves and we can be disappointed in anyone. There are streets in the way of our lives, like the ones the two disciples crossed when they were going to Emmaus. The whole reality they were relying on collapsed in a few moments and sadness replaced any other alternative perspective. Remember, there are always such moments in our lives.

I would like to take C.S. Lewis reasoning on: *"He lived and let others live."* This is a very big thing. But I want to be available to do more than that. **"Let's live and help others live."** This is the highest step and duty of any Christian. Not only to live, help the one next to you to live, love him and accept him together with his struggles and depressions.

CHAPTER 3. What is Depression?

"I felt strange and deep doubts struggling inside me," Walt Whitman.

Depression is a significant mood disorder and its manifestation is different from person to person. It is important to note that not all people who struggle with depression experience the same range of symptoms or the same intensity. [9]

The intensity and severity of depression may vary on a continuum (see Figure 3.1), at one end of which there may be mild or moderate symptoms, such conditions as: *increased sadness, irritability, loss of appetite and energy, sleep problems. At the other end of the continuum there may be more severe symptoms such as: difficulty concentrating, prolonged fatigue, isolation from those around us, feelings of despair, suicidal* behavior and *thoughts.* [10]

I feel sad. Do I have depression?

An important distinction deserves to be made between states close to depression, such as **sadness**.

Sadness is a negative, natural but functional emotion that occurs when we experience difficult events, especially those we consider loss (loss of a meaningful relationship, a good opportunity, or a certain status).

The main differences between sadness and depression are the following: sadness is usually moderate and transient, while depression is persistent, lasting; sadness does not necessarily affect our own value or image of ourselves, while depression brings with it strong feelings of guilt, worthlessness, uselessness.

When we are sad, we can still feel certain positive emotions, and suicidal thoughts do not occur. Instead depression involves a diminished ability to feel joy or pleasure and suicidal thoughts can occur, as we have seen in some people of God in the previous chapter. Sadness is when you stumble and fall, but get up. Depression is when you stumble and fall, but stay on the floor.

Sadness is that uncomfortable emotion, but one that allows us to learn. The mind is more prone when it is sad to analyze things and learn important lessons from the past and present. Sadness is not an enemy, it can often be an ally, because it facilitates critical thinking. When we are happy, most of us do not feel like analyzing and possibly deducing certain mistakes we make (Ecclesiastes 7: 3).

Depression is manifested by specific symptoms and lasts for at least two weeks in which they are present, almost daily. All the specified symptoms do NOT have to be present to have depression, it is enough for only a part of them to appear. In fact, the whole rainbow of symptoms rarely appears. [11]

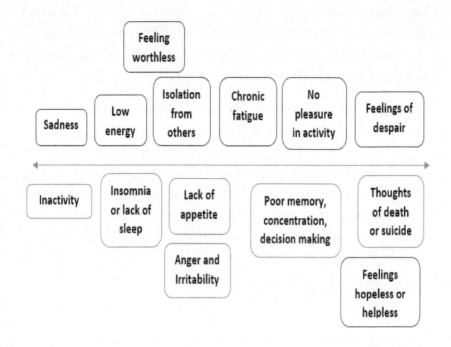

Figure 3.1.

Simply said, depression affects several aspects that I will briefly detail: *emotional, behavioral, cognitive and physiological* (at the level of the body). Depression affects the way we think, behavior, what we feel, and relationships with others, to the extent that it causes new distress but also causes an inability to function at optimal capacity. [12]

At the emotional level, when a person is depressed, negative emotions appear, such as a heightened state of sadness, loss of pleasure or interest in almost anything (things that used to fascinate us and bring fulfillment, now no longer represents any molecule of joy), or irritability (we can break out and get angry about anything).

The behavioral facet targets the main possible behaviors: agitation or motor slowness (sluggishness, slowness), isolation from others, giving up or avoiding pleasant activities, and certain suicidal attempts.

Regarding the cognitive part, a person struggling with depression may experience difficulty in concentrating (can no longer read as before, is not there, now), thoughts that devalue their own person: "I see no choice, no I am good for nothing," or pessimism: " My future will be a disaster." Also, decision making can be affected. Even small and simple decision can suffer. **At the physiological level**, may occur the following symptoms: chronic fatigue, changes in appetite, insomnia or hypersomnia, somatic pain, and tension.

Can the brain really be affected by depression?

Short and very rudimentary, the answer is yes. Studies that have used cerebral neuroimaging and scanned brain images, have shown some problems with the way certain systems involved in regulating our mood or how we feel emotions and process rewards. There are also changes in the processes of the mind, such as motivation, memory, attention, and regulation of stress response. [13]

Differences between people with depression and those without, were also identified in the structure of certain regions (volume of gray and white matter) and in their functionality (glucose consumption or the activity of certain neurotransmitters). For those who want more details in this area, can be accessed from the references section. Therefore, there is undisputed evidence and fingerprints that the harshness and density of life can affect the brain in an extremely unpleasant way. [14]

Can depression wear a mask?

If she couldn't until now, we did our best to make her adapt. At one point I was talking to someone who explained to me with great passion and ardor that depression in the countryside does not dare to appear. There are no such symptoms here, he told me. Later, researching the problem, I realized he was right, there are no such symptoms there, because there are others to which they turned.

Depression "takes shape" depending on how it is allowed to express itself in that area. The depression in the countryside is expressed differently from the one in the town. If we explore the problem further, we will find that every culture or region has an "accepted way" in which depression can be expressed.

For example, in India, mental problems are seen as a defect that cannot be told to a doctor or relatives. That is why patients who have depression when they go to the doctor report certain pains in their body, because they are accepted and tolerated there.

In Zimbabwe, depression is called "kufungisisa" which means "overthinking." In Korea there is "accumulated fire syndrome," the main symptoms being abdominal pain, sighing, impulsive walking, emotional discharge, moaning, etc. [15]

Let me simplify things for you. In Christian culture, because we exile depressive states to the corner of the ring, they may express themselves a little differently, depending on how we perceive that it is okay to happen. This is called *somatization*.

When the pain in the mind reaches its maximum, the body takes over that pain and converts it into symptoms that we know better: chest pain, palpitations, pain in the heart area, and frequent headache. Remember that stomachache that came on suddenly when you were very upset? But those sweats that seemingly have nothing to do with it? What about palpitations? I won't mention "fatigue for no reason."

There are studies that show that chronic pain, which apparently has no objective reasons, may be closely related to our mood. [16] Attention, I don't want to confuse things, we're talking about somatization when the physical causes of other potential diseases have been eliminated.

Somatization or masking depression occurs due to the fact that we constantly try to stifle pain or deny it, running away from emotional problems. And when the glass fills up, we all know what's going on. After all, how long can you swim through the turbulent waters?

This sad reality is described by the sons of Korah (Psalm 42) but also in the book of Psalms and Proverbs by King David and later by the wise Solomon.

"When I kept silence, my bones waxed old through my roaring all the day long," Psalms 32:3.

"A merry heart doeth good like a medicine; but a broken spirit drieth the bones," Proverbs 17:22

Each unpaid emotional bill costs a lot and in the end, our well-being and health is the full payment. It is important to pay these bills, because by denying their existence, they will not disappear by themselves, but will get worse with each postponed day. Pretending, in the end, costs more than the accepting the truth.

I know what depression is because I've been through depression

In clinical practice ordinarily, I attract the majority of patients who are diagnosed with major depressive disorder. I think I'm destined to be a magnet for depression. When such a case arose, I deserved it. This is what the good God allowed. I always listened reverently to the story of depression from patients, but I understood it when it was my turn to live it.

You understand depression best when you experience depression. However, I do not necessarily encourage you to live it. It is extremely difficult to understand a person who reports some common symptoms if you have never felt them. Some time ago, I experienced a situation that completely destabilized my perspective on the world and life. Immediately after the shock of those problems, there were some known symptoms that I had never expected. I started to feel very sad all day long. I didn't have a gram of energy for absolutely anything and every day I received, I saw it as a punishment, not as an opportunity.

If I could sleep, I couldn't tell if I was dreaming, sleeping, or was awake. My mind was running all sorts of unfortunate scenarios. Before I used to do sports, I really liked the movement, I read and studied quite a lot, I played the guitar and I had many other hobbies. By the time these symptoms appeared, all the pleasant activities before, had completely disappeared, there was no question of such thing.

My ability to concentrate was so stunted that when I tried to read something, my mind was no longer there. I couldn't really assimilate what I was reading, no matter how wonderful was the reading. When I got up from my knees in

33

prayer, it was as if I had never gotten on my knees. Future plans? The only reasonable plan was to have no plan. Going to church and listening about joy, and all stuff were endless chores. When I could avoid them, I did it with great skill.

There was no question of having any more pleasure in singing, and the food had begun to taste like sadness and depression. Any experience I lived, whether: I saw, heard, imagined, thought, remembered: everything was contaminated by the black clouds of depression. All the strange and deep doubts were piling up inside me.

Now those moments seem so far away and erased. But God wanted to teach me a lesson. I accepted it very hard and I felt it even harder. The braver we are, the harder we will feel the collapse in its time. And the lesson is simple: collapse has its time, no matter who you are and how strong we think we are (Ecclesiastes 3: 1).

Don't start diagnosing

In human nature there is a desire to label, judge and diagnose. The reason I wrote about these indicators is to help us identify depression, not to be undercover diagnoses. Once you have identified certain issues, this chapter achieves its goal. It is not everyone's job to determine the diseases and make a diagnosis. There are specialized people who study the problem, know how it manifests, and whom God has placed beside us, to accurately accomplish this mission. So don't diagnose yourself or others.

CHAPTER 4. The Causes of Depression

"By knowing certain things, we realize what we do not know."

One of the most common questions when we in pain is: Why? Why me?

I have heard dozens of such questions from patients, shot down by the arrows of depression. It's like a disk that once turned on doesn't stop. Even when we have a deep knowledge of things, this seed sprouts in our minds: Why do these things happen to me? Why can't it be easy?

The answer to this question is a complex and nuanced one, but it is extremely important to process the cause of the problems, because depending on this perspective, we will act in one way or another. Therefore, we will make a brief incursion into what the literature tells us about the cause of these problems, and finally we will see what God's Word says about this.

The vast majority of diseases do not have a single cause, they involve an accumulation of reasons. Formulated in simpler terms, a glass of water is compound of many drops of water. Therefore, depression involves a combination of factors that interact with each other. [17]

1.Biological factors

There are studies that show that people who develop depression come with a genetic background that makes them vulnerable to it. Each of us has the 5HTTLPR (serotonin transporter gene) which has a short or long form. People who have inherited the short form from their parents are more vulnerable to depression. In other words, they have a higher sensitivity to negative events, compared to those who chose the long form of this gene. Attention, sensitivity, not depression. [18]

This gene is related to the mood we have. If serotonin levels are high, the mood tends to be good, but if it drops significantly, we begin to feel depressed.

If we look at those around us, we will find that in a natural and mysterious way, some of us are more inclined to be sad no matter what happens, others are happy and laugh out of any stupidity or because today is Monday. This is how the Creator of Heaven and Earth decided to differentiate us.

The main idea worth remembering here is that some of us are built and created to be more sensitive than others, in terms of how we project painful events. But it does not mean we will necessarily develop depression, but we will be more vulnerable.

2.Psychological factor

In this category we encounter different things related to our mind, for example the thoughts and scenarios we run. Sometimes when we have to deal with considerable losses (someone dear, the job, an important friendship, the emotional support), we have the feeling we did not do as expected.

I have often noticed in clinical practice the appearance of hopelessness. That idea that I exhausted all the options I saw available. As in the case of King David, God no longer seems to be there with us. *Is He really still there?* However, these biological and psychological factors are risk factors (vulnerabilities). They may explain some of the depressive symptoms, but they are not direct causes of depression. [19]

Then what are the direct causes?

1.Behavioral theory was introduced by Peter M. Lewinsohn (1974) who states that depressive mood occurs because in our environment there is a low rate of positive reinforcement associated with our behavior. [20] The situation we have reached does not give us enough rewards and joy for a few simple reasons:

We have a poor social environment: for example, we lose a loved one (mother, father, friend, husband / wife). This means we automatically no longer receive the encouragement or all the benefits of that relationship. Some are born into such environment devoid of affection, support and empathy, a context that does not provide the necessary reinforcements and resources.

We do not have the skills and abilities to get the necessary reinforcements. If you are a more withdrawn, shy and angry person, you are usually more isolated from family, people, friends, colleagues. Someone simply said, "I don't really know how to make friends and be friend."

Inability to process reinforcements. I don't know how to pay attention and enjoy the good, pleasant things in my life. I don't know how to let them flood my mind, but instead I know how to be very sensitive to the negative ones. Moreover, I tend to interpret neutral events as negative (for example, someone gives me attention and care and I consider that he does it because he wants something from me).

Social strengthening of depression. It appears when those around me pay a lot of attention to me, because I am sad, they call me, they invite me to a coffee, because I feel bad. From here the mind learns that it is convenient to have depression, until those around us get tired of depression.

2.Cognitive theory of depression

It was introduced by the psychiatrist A. Beck (1967, 1983, 2008), being considered one of the best supported theories with scientific evidence. [21] The key factor in this theory is the importance of our thoughts and beliefs. The human mind begins to encode different beliefs and perspectives early in life. In other words, depression is mainly caused by the attitudes and beliefs we have formed throughout our lives, which are activated by the events we are currently facing (see figure 4.1).

From an early age we go through various more or less unpleasant contexts that favor the formation of beliefs: stable, strong, and inflexible. [22] In most situations, the mind has not really processed the importance and effect of those events on us. For example, if I was humiliated at school and had repeated failures there, my mind can learn that " I don't care much anyway, I'm not good enough, I'm a total failure, or the only one to blame for all the disasters in my life." These beliefs are strongly fixed in the mind and come to the surface in today's difficulty times, for example if I was humiliated or failed an important exam.

These beliefs have never really been addressed and resolved. Later, through them, depression creeps into our lives. When you start to think that you are not good enough, you even find evidence of this and later "black dogs of depression" appear. [23]

If these beliefs are not activated at the moment, we live by camouflaging them without bothering us much. Instead if they are hooked by certain troubles, they can lead to distortions of reality and later to depression. The moment these schemes are active, the mind begins the battle of distorting reality. What this theory proves is that the situation itself does not lead to depression.

It is not the fact that we are going through trouble that pushes us into the arms of depression, but the way our minds think about these situations. The way we project trouble into our minds makes us feel depressed, sad, worried, and so on.

To make it easier to understand, think that 50 people go through the same situation (find out that they have a few more months to live) but do they all react the same way? Not at all. They react according to the beliefs they have in mind. Some of them will be devastated and surrender ("it's all over for me"), *others will be sad but will make plans for* those months ('I haven't finished my life yet"), others will rejoice in a sad nuance that they can finish their run well ("I have lived as many days as God has given to me and I have lived them well").

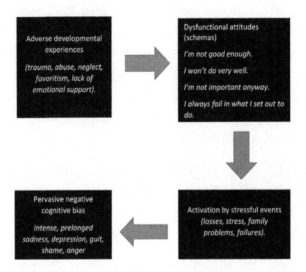

Figure 4.1

If you want an interesting challenge, try to identify what God's people thought about their troubles. You will be very surprised by some differences.

To summarize, the way we think about what is happening to us is much more important than what is happening.

Depression as an opportunity. What does the Bible tell us about depression?

"And not only so, but we glory in tribulations also, knowing that tribulation worketh patience and pacience, experience and experience, hope" Romans 5:3,4,5.

Depression is often seen by us Christians as a punishment or as something to be denied, hidden, buried deep. But in reality it is really an opportunity. It sounds hard to accept but depression has the role of shaping our character and fostering our ascension. It's not a punishment, it's a huge opportunity.

The apostle Paul sees trouble (depression, anxiety, loss, beatings) as the only ways to develop our minds. There is no other way. The chains of remarkable change in our lives begin when trouble and suffering begin. It makes sense to endure trouble because it will be fully rewarded. So, the cause is actually our growth. You may feel confused reading this though and wonder how it is possible.

The first benefit of suffering is patience. Patience is one of the great virtues that God requires from us. Trouble teaches us to be gentler with ourselves, to learn to tolerate difficult times as part of our lives. The second benefit is victory. Do you want to be patient? To become victorious? The answer is trouble. With patience and learning in suffering, we will know how to overcome and become more like the image of the Lord Jesus.

The last great benefit is hope. The victories engraved in our heart form the mentality and beliefs we have. A strong mentality knows how to go through suffering, it becomes unbalanced, but it is precisely because of these problems that it reaches the maturity required by God.

Why do troubles and depressions sometimes occur in our lives? I call it the ruthless triad of opportunities: **patience-victory-hope.** Ruthless because it brings opportunities only by suffering. We would often like to have a lot of patience, we always dreamed of winning and we would like to have a lot of hope. But it all happens because of the suffering. If we eliminate the trouble from this equation, we have eliminated everything.

James, the brother of Jesus, continues the reasoning described by the apostle Paul. The crown of life. The crown of life will be given only to those who will endure, trouble, temptation, trial. And who among us would not want to receive the crown of life that God has promised to those who love Him?

"Knowing this, that the trying of your faith worketh patience. Blessed is the man that endureth temptation for when he is tried, he shall receive the crown of life, which Lord hath promised to them that love him" James 1:3, 12.

Depression brings with it the opportunity to learn about the problems of the mind and to make various corrections where is required to completely change our minds, as God wills. Depression brings with it the moment of cleanliness. Trouble has not only short-term benefits (patience, victory, hope) but also long-term, the crown of life if we are patient and are found good.

If at this moment you are down and you think you do not have the strength to get up, do not forget that God allows all things to bring us closer to Him. Even a ruthless disease like depression. One of the roles of depression is to shape our character, but it should NEVER be meant to destroy us.

When there is no connection between what you do and what happens to you

When we strive to be close to God and do our job well, we automatically set certain expectations in our mind. We expect to receive good, because we do good (Genesis 4:7). When we offer respect, we expect to receive respect. If we are faithful, we expect others to be faithful. If we are honest, we think that the others will be the same and so it will be good. If we love, we expect others to love us and it will be good. But this is not always the case. In fact, the miracle rarely happens.

You look around and notice all kinds of wicked, unjust, unfaithful people. And they are respected, they are doing great and they are making good progress. Those who have done good receive evil, and those who have done evil receive good. And then you start to see no connection between what you do and what you receive.

All the meaning you had is gone. Automatically what we do starts to have no value. Everything I did, I did in vain. And so, the depression begins to creep into our minds. Any of us can get to the point where we no longer understand the meaning of things.

Martin Seligman studied this phenomenon called learning helplessness. [24] Do you learn that whatever you do does not bring you results and then what is the point of doing anything else?

In one of his studies he put some dogs in a cage that had 2 gates. If they walked through one of the gates, they received an electric shock, on the other they received food. Simpler than that: *a punishment or a reward*. Being smart animals, they learned not to go where they received the electric shock, but where they received food.

At some point, the experimenter changed the conditions. When they went where they used to receive shocks, sometimes they received food, sometimes electric shocks. When they went where they first received food, sometimes they received electric shocks, sometimes food. In a random form. What happened?

The animals became more and more apathetic and gradually began to retreat and no longer want to walk through either of the 2 gates. Even though there were no restrictions, the dogs gave up any possible option, some of them preferring death.

When you press the right button but receive a lot of punishment, the mind loses its meaning and gradually reaches the end of its powers. Any healthy mind works this way.

PART TWO.

o Is it enough to pray and wait for things to

work out on their own?

o Is there anything to be done to improve

things?

o What can I do to be victorious in the fight against

Depression?

CHAPTER 5. Treatment of Depression

"Your observation is good. Maybe too good. That's why I tend to oppose it." [25]

It's a big disappointment for me when I hear different voices saying something like, _"Pray for this." Just give it to God, Only God can solve this."_ In fact, when we say that, we are saying that we are the ones who fail miserably to address such an issue. Do not misunderstand me, there is nothing wrong or bad for someone to pray for recovery from a mental illness, on the contrary it is one of the things that saves us.

We know that prayer is the way to connect with God. We need to pray constantly. But would you say to someone who has cancer, diabetes, or heart problems and needs surgery to pray and just give everything to God? Would you tell him that the only viable solution is God? I hope you would tell him that, but don't forget to mention that it would be advisable to see a doctor as well.

This is what the Lord Jesus states in 3 of the 4 Gospels in Holy Scripture: _"When Jesus heard it, he said to them, those who are healthy have no need for a physician, but those who are sick do"_ _Matthew 9:12_ The main idea that emerges from this verse is that the sick person needs a doctor! Consequently, it is biblical to treat yourself if you have some problems. God has changed and healed many problems of the mind. God works the way He wants, in His terms and often using the specialized people around us. For this reason, it is advisable to have a perspective that does not push us towards falling, but towards peace of mind and soul.

How patients with depression are treated

According to guidelines from the American Psychiatric Association (APA, 2010) and the National Institute for Health and Care Excellence, in the United Kingdom (Nice, 2011) [26], there are two forms of treatment for this disorder and they can be used independently or in combination: **psychotherapy and pharmacotherapy** (antidepressant medication).

Medication treatment

The main function of antidepressants is to adjust the balance of certain neurotransmitters such as serotonin, norepinephrine or dopamine, which we know are responsible for how we feel emotionally. [27] The effect of the medication appears after about 2-4 weeks and the major improvements appear in terms of sleep, appetite, ability to concentrate and mood.

There are several classes of antidepressants, but I will mention just a few so as not to burden the reader's mind with much specialized information: serotonin reuptake inhibitors (SSRIs), serotonin and norepinephrine reuptake inhibitors (SNRIs), tricyclic antidepressants. For more details go to the references section. [28]

Unfortunately, there is no evidence to support that these positive effects of treatment are maintained over time. [29] Moreover, guidelines (APA, 2012) show that the positive effects of medication are maintained only if it is not stopped. Other serious studies show that antidepressant medication works better in cases of severe depression, not for mild or moderate cases. [30] Even if medications attack depression at the level of symptoms by balancing neurotransmitters, is an option that should not be neglected, especially in cases where depression has a severe form.

Psychotherapy

It is an effective alternative treatment and is recommended as the first line of treatment in most guidelines for treating depression. The ideal choice would be the combination of medication and psychotherapy, which proves to be the most effective solution. [31]

Psychotherapy is the complex process in which we learn how certain things work in our minds and what we can do to change them. In this process we learn ways to change and counteract thoughts and how to improve mood. We also learn how to fight with those beliefs that cause negative emotions, and how to develop positive emotions, how to identify effective solutions to solve the problems which are stronger than us or what we can do to relax the mind and the body.

The Bible teaches that our purpose is to do whatever we can to obey Christ. We have a duty to overthrow inventions of the mind (2 Corinthians 10: 5). A psychiatrist, psychotherapist, or counselor who has a biblical view and valuable knowledge of the mind, can help you learn exactly how you can do this. In other words, we all know that it is not necessarily useful to worry excessively, but how many of us still achieve such a performance? How many of us really don't worry too much? By modifying these components with effort and involvement, the mind eventually comes to equilibrate the chemical balance and prevent future problems.

Think that all your life, you have traveled on a path full of problems, some you created with your own hands, others appeared without being directly involved and the brain drew different patterns and makes various predictions in the way you see things and you relate to them. You have traveled and smoothed this route for years. With the help of psychotherapy you learn to give up that path and choose another way of approaching things, find another new path to follow. So psychotherapy is nothing but a form of learning, nothing mystical about it.

Do you remember the metaphor of the carpet under which all sorts of filth lies? In counseling or therapy the carpet is set aside and the restructuring and reshaping of the mind begins to achieve the purpose for which we were created. This will help you to have a safer and a protected place inside your mind to help you in the battles that will follow. Our mind was created to be a dear place to be, not a room of endless torture: *"I am came that they may have life and may have it abundantly."* John 10:10. So, give me some credit and let's practice a little psychotherapy.

CHAPTER 6. Behavioral Activation

" Enough had been thought, and said, and felt, and imagined.
It was about time that something should be done" C.S. Lewis.

On a cold and too soon morning, I took the elevator to the 3 glorious floors that led to the Psychiatry Department. I had enough energy and could not wait to see what patients were there in that day. I have shown my intention to take a case of severe depression, because as you well know, for a reason or another I am like a magnet that attracts depression. I just can't help it. I was told that I had to go to Mrs. M and do behavioral activation with her.

Said and done, I thought, it doesn't seem to be beyond me. I knew the theory well. But as I would find out later, I was terribly mistaken. I picked up a list of fun activities, walked into the salon, and headed for the patient. Mrs. M was lying on her back in bed, with her eyes fixed on the ceiling. She had that look that tells you from the start to finish the therapies quickly and to mind your own business.

I presented myself briefly and I told her what my intentions were and the result was no answer. I encouraged her to tell me a few things about herself and what the current issues were. The answers, if they can be considered answers, were vague, monosyllabic and lifeless. When I asked her what she liked to do before, the final answer was something like that, "I don't remember anything."

I asked her about family, children, grandchildren, flowers, friends; absolutely everything my mind could think of in that situation. That's what she did all day. She sat in bed staring at the ceiling. When I asked her what she was thinking about, the unwanted, short and sharp answer came immediately: nothing.

Now her mind had wiped out all the pleasant things in her life, there was nothing that convinced her to do anything. She couldn't talk to me and after 10 minutes I realized she was very tired and wanted me to leave. I negotiated the "conditions of my departure," a 3-meter walk and slowly left the salon. I considered it a defeat. I left the salon with all the tires deflated, including the spare one. I later found out that this is the case for almost all patients who have severe depression. No reaction. But we don't need to get there. There is another option.

Why are things getting worse?

When we feel depressed we tend to avoid activities that tire us. We believe that they will make us even more tired and that we will register new failures. So, there are two big threats. *Inactivity* and *avoidance*. The problem is we not only avoid difficult activities but we also avoid the pleasant, recreational ones that we used to do, because we feel that we don't like them anymore and there is no point in doing them anymore.

We actually avoid getting involved in activities that would bring us results, we avoid doing behaviors that would have positive states and we avoid doing things that make sense to us. Basically, we avoid everything we can avoid: people, negative emotions, thoughts, plans or making decisions. Massive avoidance I call it.

The consequences are dramatic. For example, if I isolate myself from everyone and I don't meet anyone because I feel depressed, the consequence is that I will feel more and more lonely and I deduce that no one cares about me. Moreover, I avoid others until they avoid me. And this is exactly how we stepped into the vicious circles of avoidance.

The bottom line is that what we feel often comes from what we do. If you behave like a man who has depression, you will feel like a man who has depression. And the mind promotes a distorted theory: *"When the depressions are over, I will resume my activities."*Nothing is more wrong. The longer we wait for the state to change without doing anything, the longer the depression lasts and takes shape in us.

Take a sheet of paper and a sharp pencil and write down what activities you have completed in the last few days, what activities you have avoided and how they have made you feel. Evaluate how you felt from 0 (very bad) to 10 (very good, excellent). Consequently, the problem is getting worse for two central reasons: *we avoid activities that would give us good results, positive emotions and significance;* **and** *we live according to emotional states, not according to the values and goals God has given to us.*

Why do we do behavioral activation?

Through behavioral activation we reduce depression and regain the meaning of living. According to recent studies summarized by Leahy 2017, behavioral activation has remarkable effects in reducing the symptoms of depression. [32]

Behavioral activation refers to the fact that we plan and perform repeated actions even if we feel bad. There are only two alternatives: **to live life on the depressive function or to live life in an antidepressant way.** We can admit we feel very sad, we accept that these are the problems but we do completely differently than depression tells us. Despite the fact that depression tells us there is nothing interesting to do, we make plans and apply them.

It is normal for things to be difficult at first, our actions to overwhelm us and our depression to stop us. But gradually, patiently, continuing to perform them, will become more natural, easier to perform and depression will diminish. Through repeated and systematic **ACTION** we change the depressive mood. If you were used to reading the book of Revelation intensively for hours before, do not begin with the book of Revelation now, change things up and pick another one right from the start of the New Testament.

Antidepressant actions

Actions that have the power to fight with depression have 3 major characteristics: they make us feel better, they make sense to us and ultimately help us achieve good results. The moment we start deliberately planning these actions, the chances of completing them increase significantly.

How to proceed?

Choose a certain place and a specific time of the day to plan your actions for the next day. Let's say evening. Make this planning a good, holy habit. Take a sheet of paper and a pen and write down the activities you want to do the next day. Most likely depression will tell you to do few activities and at long intervals. You have the right to be rebellious in this matter. Do not listen to that voice. Write down the actions in the simplest and clearest terms possible. This will help you accomplish each and every one of them easier.

For instance: *To wake up and read a short passsage from the Bible, to pray, to meet a dear brother, practice the guitar, to listen my favorites songs, to plant a tree in the garden, ride a bike, read a great book, pay attention to nature, go out and do good to someone that needs it more than I do, to cook something good, to go to the church to pray, to hug the loved ones, to knit, to compose a poem, to look at old photos, to drink coffee and to feel its strong smell and fascinating taste, or to go to work.*

You can build your own list. Start with things that are neither too heavy nor too simple, appropriate and realistic. Once you have a list of what you like, schedule each activity at a specific time. For example: I wake up at 7 o'clock, read a passage from the Bible and pray until 8 o'clock, from 8-9 o'clock I cook pancakes for the family, and from 9 to 5 I go to work.

Principle to be respected with holiness

Once you have planned the actions, there is nothing to reflect or discuss or negotiate. First you execute, then you feel. You don't have to feel like you want to do them. You just need to execute them no matter if there are feelings of uselessness, fatigue, despair, or helplessness. Most of the time, you will feel that you can't do them and you don't like them. It is normal when we are depressed. ***The reasoning is simple: we do and then gradually we get to feel***. The studies we have, show us that a repetition of at least 3 weeks is needed for the symptoms of depression to decrease in intensity and frequency. [33]

The Biblie and behavioral activation

First of all, I will mention just one verse. The Holy Bible encourages us to act. Let us do whatever we do for the Lord

54

and with all our heart. Be careful, let's do it, not necessarily feel it:

'And whatever you do, work heartily, as for the Lord, and not for men," Colossians 3:23.

Prayer and Action

In Psalm 13 we can notice the man after his God heart, King David, in two very different ways. In the first part we are told about a man who has a soul full of worries and a heart full of troubles. The winner over Goliath, forgotten and abandoned for this time, is almost on his knees in front of other giants. However, in the second part of this writing we see that David puts all his problems before God. He remembers that God is in control of all things. From a depressed David, he radically changes his mood into a cheerful-hearted man who sings. Interesting contradiction, isn't it?

The idea I want to highlight here is a simple one. We need to give depression, anger, or grief a chance to leave our minds. David feels depressed, but does two essential things: **1. He comes before God to talk to Him; 2. He writes about his problems**. You can write your own epistles and God will take them into account. As a result of his contact with God and his behavioral activation, his mood changes so much that you find it hard to believe it is being discussed about the same person.

The principle of behavioral activation is also supported by the apostle Peter who writes the following:

"Therefore prepare your minds for action." 1 Peter 1:13.

When depression creeps into our minds, the arguments become weak, unimportant, and extremely difficult to penetrate. Emotions become so intense that they can bring down any reasoning no matter how noble it is. Now the main arguments that have an effect are the actions. Allow the pain to leave your mind. Pray for God to direct your steps toward meaningful activities that bring true satisfaction. He has prepared in advance the good deeds or actions to be initiated.

Therefore: STOP with reflection and **START** with action!

CHAPTER 7. Positive Emotion

"Two people looked outside through the prison gates. One saw the mud, the other saw the stars."

In previous chapters I have tried to emphasize an important aspect. Depression is not always a bad thing. Sometimes God can allow such states in our minds, just to warn us that the direction we are going is not the right one. And so we begin to become more sensitive to changing certain wrong paths in our lives. The role of depression is not to frighten or destroy us, but to communicate loud and clear: *Hey, something is wrong. IT'S TIME TO MAKE ORDER IN YOUR MIND!*

Depression and negative emotions

Without being aware, depression begins to gently distort the way we look at ourselves, at reality around us and at our future. Gradually we feel worse and worse. The main problem is the negative aspects are very big and thick in our minds, and the positive aspects are minimized to non-existent.

Good successes and experiences tend to lose their beauty or value. It is as if we were looking through thick lenses that show us as clearly as possible what is bad and definitely hide what is good. This creates an emotional imbalance, in which negative states have a much stronger impact than positive ones. Evil begins to become stronger than good and sadness more intense than joy. Our mission is to rebalance our emotions. That is why the Bible constantly encourages us to rejoice. "Rejoice always." 1 Thess. 5:16

The benefits of positive emotions

So, our mission is to get our emotion on the right track again. The difficulty arises from the fact that this correction is not made by words we usually whisper to ourselves when we are depressed: *"Look at the full side of the glass."* The words are extraordinary but at this stage they are not enough.

Our mind knows what she needs to see, but our emotions prevent her from doing so. Therefore, balancing is done through actions, as opposed to those that depression tell us to do. Simply put, what we have to do is write in our minds with the biggest and deepest letters, the good and pleasant aspects of our lives. When we start doing this, the positive emotions will counterbalance the effect of the negative ones and the intensity of the depression will decrease. [34]

Another advantage of positive emotions is that it gives us the strength to be more resilient to negative life experiences. When we go through trials they give us meaning and purpose to fight for. When we feel good, the mind frees itself from burdens and allows us to be more creative and find beauty in the mundane things we have overlooked until then. [35]

One last benefit that I want to highlight is that positive emotions help us recover faster from experiencing negative emotions and regulate the functioning of our body. Through them the mind gets rid of those bad and torturous thoughts and thus gradually we eliminate avoidance behaviors.

There are several ways in which we can regain the emotional balance and with God's help I would like to detail very briefly, those that have a solid scientific support. [36]

Cultivating the pleasures of life

Nowhere in the Bible is it said to cultivate depression and sadness. We have divine permission to feel pleasure on this Earth. Pleasure comes in principle from the sensations we feel: smells, taste, touches, and images. *You actually feel the pleasure. Pleasure is not something you're talking about, instead it's something you feel.* And I don't mean that unbridled pleasure that comes from committing iniquities. I am referring to PERMITTED activities, concrete, fine, endorsed by Scripture. Molecules of joy, left by God himself. Those types of activities that can reduce depression or make it much more bearable. There are two rules when we want to cultivate the pleasures of life: **to cultivate them as often as possible** and *to be aware of them when we cultivate them.*

 For example, if we look at a sunset, let us have our attention focused there, on what we see, on the wonderful sensations of pleasure that derive from that beautiful image, left by the Creator for the pupils of our eyes. Let's be there, enjoying the intense, reddish, bright shades without contaminating the sunset with various types of plans and thoughts. In other words, it is fundamental to be there when the joy is about to begin. The central idea is simple, FREQUENTLY and CONCENTRATED.

How exactly do we proceed?

The first step is to make a list of activities that produce sensations of pleasure. It can be completed whenever we discover something that is significantly pleasing to us. For example, some concrete activities can be: enjoying a tea alone, drinking a coffee on the terrace, touching the delicate petals of a flower and slowly smelling the inviting scent, drawing, working the land in the garden, etc.

The second step is to choose a pleasant activity every day and to do it. For example, choose to enjoy a cup of coffee in peace.

The third step is fundamental. Dedicate your body and soul to that activity when you do it as if it were your last. Try to remove any disturbance by turning off the phone, postponing any other activity. The activity needs to be carried out slowly, leisurely, giving it the necessary time. At this point it is time to stop and KNOW who the Lord is.

From time to time, stop so you can become aware of the sensations you are experiencing. For example, pour the coffee into the cup slowly, listening to the sound of its flow, notice the brown color and describe it in your mind. Smell the coffee. What does it suggest to you? Feel its warmth, sip it slowly from the cup. What do you feel in your mouth? What does it remind you of? Focus on the cup in your hand, look at its color, weigh its weight and appreciate the quality of the material.

If we do an activity that is pleasant, but our mind is elsewhere when we do it, the pleasure felt is weak and minimal and its encoding in memory is very weak. But when we dedicate ourselves to her, we live it intensely and keep it in mind for a long time.

After finishing the activity for a few minutes, remember the sensations you experienced. Were they pleasant? Review them. Recalling produces an intense and strong coding in the mind.

Use that good mood to engage in useful activities. In order for the benefits to be significant, the exercise must be practiced as often as possible and whenever deemed appropriate.

Reach out a helping hand to the tired one

No matter how sad we feel now, the truth is that there is someone sadder and tighter next to us. One of the most beautiful features of mankind is described in the pages of Scripture: *"Bear one another's burderns, and so fulfill the law of Christ,"* Galatians 6:2.

When we take care of those who are sadder than us, our well-being automatically increases, we feel useful and fulfilled. Moreover, charity is not just a well-defined command, **but one of our most feared antidotes against depression.** [37]

When we feel stuck in personal problems, and are overwhelmed by depressive states, we have the impression that the world is only nuanced in an unwelcome black. Thus we conclude that there is not much left to do for us. However, by doing good to others, we are able to expand our horizons of the world and gain another meaning of our worth and actions. Helping someone else helps ourselves. I realize that at first glance it may sound slightly selfish, but that's how the mind really works. [38]

Alfred Adler, a psychiatrist, often used this approach with patients: "Try to think every day about how you can help someone." When your thoughts don't let you fall asleep, you can think about how you can help somebody. What burden can you take from other's shoulders?

The reasoning is as biblical as possible. By giving, we receive. *"It is more blessed to give than to receive"* Acts 20:35. By helping someone in distress, sadness and self-pity diminish. We feel better and we are reborn with every step we take. [39]

How do we proceed?

Force yourself to do a good deed at least once a week. It could be a stranger, a dear friend, a family member, someone poorer than you, or a simple colleague. Voluntarily, do something that you know brings joy to that person. Think about the good you bring to the other person and buy him a coffee on the way to work. Or even better, make coffee at home with great pleasure and offer it with love to someone in need.

Notice the expression that stirs that person's face when you have made them happy. What words are addressed to you? What emotions did you produce? How does it make you feel? It is important to learn to do good in an authentic way, without expecting anything in return.

Unearthing the repressed passions

Another way to cultivate great joy involves expressing a repressed passion. A repressed passion is a certain action or activity, which I once learned, but for various reasons (lack of appreciation, lack of support) I gave up achieving it. Perform an analysis on activities that in the past gave you a lot of meaning and excited you a lot, that energized you and made you dream but that you gave up, either because you did not have enough time or you were discouraged from different points of view.

Perhaps you want the desire to play an instrument or paint on fine canvas. Maybe you buried something you never got to do, even though it would have been a huge pleasure. Do your best to dig after those repressed desires. Maybe at some point you would have liked to travel a lot but you didn't have the money. Or you may have wanted to learn how to make amazing cakes at some point, but you didn't have the support and context. You may have always wanted to learn to parachute, but you didn't have the courage. Now is the right time. Which of your passions could you pursue at this point in your life?

How do we proceed?

The first step is to think of a repressed passion and write it down carefully.

The second step is to draw up an action plan. This implies a solution for practicing this passion. What materials do you need? From where can you get them?

The third step is to allocate time and practice it, and following that you will ultimately think and write down those states that the practice of this exercise awakens in you.

God created positive emotions

When the Creator built the human mind, he endowed it with various abilities. One of them is to feel the joy fully and leisurely. So it is allowed to rejoice. Dare!

A day when we cannot afford to feel at least a molecule of joy and fascination, is a day when we directly violate biblical principles. It is a wasted day as lived under the standards of the Creator.

So there are several types of exercises through which we can develop positive emotions to overcome depression. These include cultivating the pleasures of life, extending a helping hand to people who are tired, or digging up from repressed passions. You can choose the ones that suit you and practice them constantly. Through repetition, over time you will achieve effective results and states that are to your advantage.

CHAPTER 8. Maximizing Sleep Quality

"In peace I will both lay myself down and sleep, for you, Yahweh alone, make me live in safety." Psalms 4:8

Often sleep problems are related to depression. The main difficulties in maintaining quality sleep in depression are: *hypersomnia* and *insomnia*. Sometimes they are present as symptoms of depression or may be a precursor to depression. The worsening of sleep problems sabotages the body and prevents it from acquiring the resources necessary for optimal functioning.

Sleep problems also have an impact on how our clarity in making decisions works. [40] When the quality of sleep suffers, many problems can appear such as: difficulty concentrating and problems with attention, memory, increased irritability, somatic pain, poor performance at work, anxiety or depression. [41] Healthy sleep has multiple benefits, including: *a lower risk of developing depression, contributes to a rapid acceleration in the relief of depressive symptoms and reduces the risk of recurrence of depressive symptoms after they have diminished.*

The importance of increased investigation

If it is very difficult for you to have a restful sleep, in addition to the specialized recommendations offered in this chapter, it is crucial to have a specialist consultation due to the fact there is a possibility that certain medical conditions may be involved in sleep problems. For example: sleep apnea, gastroesophageal reflux, and hyperthyroidism (endocrine dysfunction).

Hypersomnia and Depression

Hypersomnia is a state of prolonged drowsiness that is manifested by the persistent need to sleep during the day or by episodes of prolonged sleep. [42] Many patients who have hypersomnia, sleep too much and yet wake up as tired as they were at bedtime.

In most cases it is often accompanied by exhaustion and fatigue that are not alleviated by increasing sleep duration. The most common causes of hypersomnia are mental health problems, namely depression and anxiety. Hypersomnia can occur either before depression sets in and leads to the maintenance of depressive symptoms or after depression sets in when it begins to become a way to escape the harsh and unpleasant reality.

Instead of confronting the bad thoughts that upset us, we prefer to postpone making certain decisions or solving problems that are beyond our control. At the same time, we avoid interactions with those around us due to the fact that we do not have enough energy.

The main methods of intervention against hypersomnia are: *medical treatment (if sleep problems are persistent it is essential to contact a psychiatrist), psychological intervention (helps to acquire certain skills to help change troublesome thoughts, problem solving, decision making, and reducing insomnia).*

Insomnia and Depression

Insomnia means difficulty falling asleep and maintaining sleep. The main components that maintain insomnia are **bad habits, intense activity in the mind, thoughts that do not help us and the agitation present at the physiological level.** [43]

Sleep problems and inappropriate habits

The first unhealthy habit that affects the quality of sleep is the disorganized schedule of sleep hours. To have a good sleep it is necessary to establish a routine regarding the hours of sleep. We cannot induce sleep through a mental command but by establishing a routine, we begin to program the mind to enter a stable sleep-wake cycle. [44]

How do we proceed?

The first important step is to establish a daily routine of pre-sleep behaviors. Simply put, it is essential to build a habit that the mind will always recognize as the road to sleep. For example, we go to the toilet, brush our teeth, put on the sleep clothes, and sit in bed reflecting on 2-3 good experiences from that day and thank God for taking care of us. Create your own sleep routine.

Another extremely important aspect is to establish a bedtime and wake-up time. No matter how we feel, about 20 minutes before bedtime, start your pre-sleep routine. The mind must know that the time to rest has come. In the morning, no matter how you rested during the night, get out of bed at the appointed time. Another important component is not to sleep during the day no matter how you feel. If you sleep during the day, it is normal not to be able to fall asleep at the set time.

The second unhealthy habit is a disorganized environment. Therefore, an extremely important step is to build a good sleeping environment. Remove unnecessary noise, excessive heat and cold, uncomfortable bed or annoying lights as much as possible. For example, you can use earplugs or sleeping glasses, adjust the room temperature, or use a suitable blanket, mattress or clothing.

Another environmental factor, often overlooked, are stimulating activities that are repeatedly associated with where we sleep. All of these activities can cause insomnia. For example, watching TV while sitting in bed, surfing the Internet or laptop sitting in bed, reading in bed, or worrying in bed. By doing such activities in the bedroom, the brain comes to associate them with stimulation, not sleep. When we sit in bed, the mind automatically needs to know that it is going to rest.

How can the mind fall asleep in an environment where she repeatedly performs activities that impede sleep? If you are used to sitting in bed and instead of sleeping, debate all possible worries, the mind is unable to fall asleep, because on an unconscious level, and there are too many associations between what the mind has to do when it is in bed.

The recommendation is simple. As much as possible, use the bedroom and the bed only for sleep. The mind must associate the bedroom and the bed with rest. In time, simply entering in this environment will be enough for the mind to rest.

The last unhealthy habit is related to inadequate nutrition before bed. Quality nutrition helps to achieve quality sleep. If you are used to having such habits, there may be abdominal cramps, bloating, and difficult breathing. Digestive problems can also significantly affect the quality of sleep. It is extremely complicated to sleep well if the food consumed has not been digested adequately. The solution is to avoid very high fats, sweets, juices, coffee, or energy drinks 2-3 hours before bedtime. Alcohol and tobacco are also elements that need to be avoided, especially before sleepy time. [45]

Our thoughts and the quality of sleep

Do you often sit in bed and think about various things from the past, such as regrets or remorse? Or trying to fall asleep and criticize yourself for a failure or something you couldn't do?

In order to get a pleasant and restful sleep, you need to teach your mind to detach of certain problems and worries.

An important truth to consider is described in the Gospel of Matthew: *"Therefore don't be anxious for tomorrow, for tomorrow will be anxious for itself"* Matthew 6:34.

One of our purposes is to help the mind clearly understand that the current day is over and tomorrow will be a new day. An effective solution is to end the day by making an agenda for the next day. If the mind perceives the day is not over, it will operate in the way it works and will begin to diligently detect various problems and solutions. Once we make the plan and define the problems for the next day, we begin to release the pressure to solve them. It must be clear to the mind that today is over and tomorrow is another day.

There is a very obvious reason why sleep problems can get significantly worse, namely bad and uncontrolled thoughts. This problem is called *rumination* in the literature. More specifically, rumination occurs when we think about all thoughts. If we have accustomed our minds to make various catastrophic predictions and to react with exaggerated attitudes towards our own thoughts and states, it will be very difficult for us to fall asleep and maintain sleep. These thoughts will maximize our agitation and prevent us from resting. Moreover, we can get to the point where sleep deprivation feeds our dark thoughts, and these thoughts cause us discomfort and anxiety that sustain insomnia. When thoughts start to affect us, the mind can run various scenarios like the one below:

"If I can't sleep, it must be serious. If I don't sleep well at night, I'm sure I'll have a bad day tomorrow. I definitely have a serious medical problem! Insomnia will ruin my life and I will not be able to enjoy anything! Everyone can sleep well, except me! Why is this happening to me? There's nothing I can do to sleep better. I am doomed to always be tired!"

One of the patients I worked with over time developed sleep problems. Our purpose was to solve these problems. The main issue was he could not sleep and woke up often. From 4 o'clock he wasn't able to fall asleep again. When I did a careful examination of sleep hygiene, I found that my patient used to watch TV until he fell asleep, and did not have a routine or a stable sleep schedule.

When my client could not sleep he sat in bed and allowed his mind to be assaulted with all sorts of thoughts and emotions. It took us several months to work on this, but gradually the quality of sleep improved. Progressively, he began to concentrate much better at work, the symptoms of depression diminished and now my patient could fall asleep much easier than before. The basic idea is that we need to have order in our sleep schedule, even it requires a lot of effort.

God himself is a God of order, not disorder. When we start to work with dedication to what is holding us back, He gives us the strength and patience to overcome problems, both big and small.

Making a brief summary, in order to improve the quality of sleep it is important to spot some important components. First of all, make sure that you have healthy sleep habits and that we have formed a routine that is to our advantage. Then, it is extremely important to make sure we have a diet that does not work in our detriment.

Finally, the next goal is to learn how to win the fight against foreign, and unwanted thoughts. When we manage to develop the ability to control thoughts and relax the mind, we will feel better and the quality of our sleep will improve significantly.

CHAPTER 9. Winning The Battle With Bad Thoughts

"Our life is what our thoughts make it," **Marcus Aurelius.**

Most of the time, we tend to believe that our emotional states of sadness, guilt, shame, anxiety, and depression, are determined by unfavorable events, the behavior of others or things that are not under our control. However, between what happens and what we feel are the thoughts and interpretations of the mind.

The emotions we feel are generated and projected by our thoughts about a certain reality. Imagine the following scenario. You are dating someone you really like. As you talk to her, you realize she is not paying attention to you and shows signs of boredom and non-involvement. However, you decide to continue the conversation. *"Maybe she's very tired. She must have had a few bad days."* You feel quite calm and quiet.

After a few minutes, you start to lose your patience, you can't find your words and with sadness and bitterness you say the following: *"Why isn't she interested in me and in the conversation I'm trying to initiate? She could say several things. I knew she couldn't like me. Maybe she doesn't like my accent or the way I look. She's certainly not interested and I'm not interesting. I'll be alone all my life."*

In just a few minutes you can get to fly in a bizarre carousel of emotions that convert into each other, thanks to the interpretations you attribute to the situation. Emotions change because we think differently about the situation that is happening to us. In other words, the events we go through, activate certain thoughts in our minds and these in turn trigger our emotional reactions.

Try to simplify things. The same news told to 10 different people will most likely trigger different emotional reactions in them, depending on how they will think about that news. [46]

However, what really happens matters

I do not mean to say that situations in reality cannot be painful in themselves. Reality matters a lot but it does not determine our reactions. What I mean is that God has given to us the power to transform reality in our minds.

"Throwing down imaginations and every high thing that is exalted against the knowledge of God, and bringing every thought into captivity to the obedience of Christ," 2 Corinthians 10:5.

The problem that arises when we bring thoughts into question is that they act by highlighting certain aspects of reality and ignoring others. Some thoughts help us feel good, while others make us feel bad. The truth is many of the thoughts we have are voices that have been built since childhood, following the experiences we have about those around us. Our beliefs come either from certain experiences or from the attitudes and behavior of model people.

Not all thoughts are good for us

Below you will find some of the types of bad thoughts that can distort reality and consequently can bring negative emotions. You can go through them and focus on the ones that suit you. They will be the material for the fight against evil thoughts. [47]

1.Mind reading

It occurs when we think we know what others think and feel about us, without having enough evidence of their thoughts. We often tend to think that they have a bad perspective on us and so we end up reacting to what we imagine they are thinking, without checking how things really are. Examples: *"He certainly thinks I'm not so smart. He despises me. He doesn't like me at all. I know how he thinks about me."*

2.Global Labeling

Involves labels that denigrate, criticize oneself or others. The problem is that labels often make us feel bad but do not offer us a viable solution to specific problems. Moreover, we get stuck in solving difficult situations, being urged to put aside our goals and give up trusting in anyone. Such thoughts may sound as follows: *"He is a man of nothing. I'm a loser. I'm a failure. I am a supreme sinner. It's so stupid. I'm forgetful. I'm always careless.''*

3.Polarized Thinking (Black and White)

This kind of distorted thinking makes us see the world only in extremes. In other words, we are either good or bad, we have done something perfect or we have failed. There is no middle ground or nuance in this thinking trap. It's like looking in the color box and seeing either white or black. If we have some partial successes, we consider them as failures. The problem is we remain in a constant state of tension that often leads to great disappointments and real crusades against us and the world. This misconception often sounds like, *"If I don't always* win, I mean I'm a loser." *If it's not perfect, I did it in vain. If I'm not very happy, I'm a lost man."*

4.Catastrophizing

Do you meet people who always expect things to go wrong? This habit of thinking makes us exaggerate and distort unpleasant situations, turning them into terrible, horrible, catastrophic. No matter what happens, the scenarios are awful: *"If my husband leaves me, my life is over. If it doesn't work out, it will be an unimaginable disaster. I'm going to lose everything and it's going to be awful. I feel terrible".*

5.Overgeneralization

It is a common trap and occurs when, based on a single unpleasant incident, we derive a generally valid conclusion. Such generalizations involve the use of keywords: *never, always, nobody, everyone.* When this distortion of reality arise, we can say something like this*: "I never do anything right." I always forget everything. It only happens to me. Nobody helps me with anything."*

6.Personalization

Surely you know someone who takes upon himself the whole guilt of mankind. Even, **if we have a small part of the fault, we often fail to see all the factors involved**. If we fall into this trap, we can think, *"It's my fault I'm depressed and I deserve my fate." My relationship doesn't work because I've never been a good partner. It's my fault I didn't know how to take care of my health."*

7.Filtering

This distortion occurs when we absorb only the negative aspects of experiences and completely ignore the neutral or positive ones. In doing so, our image of life is colored only in black. For example, if we receive constructive feedback, we only retain criticism. From a series of events, we remember only the negative ones. When someone doesn't want to help us, we forget whenever they helped us.

8.Incorrect comparisons

It is one of the most common distortions and based on certain unrealistic standards, we make all kinds of comparisons with other people, looking to see who is smarter, better, more attractive than us and by comparison we end up feeling inadequate. A few thoughts like this may sound like in this way: *He is so smart. I will not achieve anything great. My girlfriend is much better oriented than me and she is always praised by others, but I'm always a such loser."*

9.Emotional reasoning

At one point I was talking to someone and she was still trying to convince herself that something bad was going to happen. In fact, nothing bad happened later when I examined the evidence. The problem was that she always allowed her emotions to guide her in interpreting reality. The only argument she had was: *"that's how I feel. If I feel that something bad will happen, it means that something bad will really happen. If I feel guilty, it means I'm really guilty. If I feel incapable, I am incapable."*

10.Should Statements

This trap of thinking involves a series of rules about how we should feel or think or behave. How exactly the others should be. Through this attitude we put a lot of pressure on ourselves and impose on ourselves some unrealistic, exaggerated standards. For example: *"I always have to do everything perfectly. All people must be righteous. Life must be extraordinary. I must to be healthy."*

Don't torture yourself

I wrote about these types of thoughts because they are often the ones that distort our perception of reality. They cause and maintain the symptoms of depression. But more than that, they are lies and untruths that do not let us sleep and to live a meaningful and fully life. All because they are lies. And the lie cannot release. The lie finally puts you on your knees. If we are not aware of them, there is a very good chance that we will become their prisoners. This means that without realizing it, they will guide and control our whole life.

The prison of thoughts

The good news is that we have the option to choose a much better alternative. William Shakespeare managed to outline this very beautiful aspect: *"Make not your thoughts your prisons."* When we know the truth, we become free. The great opportunity is that we can work to change these evil and untrue thoughts at any time. It is not necessary to live imprisoned in a jail that we have built with our own hands.

Some of the thoughts can be changed quite easily, but others require a lot of effort. Because they were put in us insistently and we carried them with us for a long time. What is relevant is we can add new ways of understanding reality, which will give us the strength to enjoy more the life we live. Therefore, our mission is to learn how to counteract bad thoughts and to learn healthy alternatives to think about.

How do we proceed? ICAR procedure

I'm not going to lie to you. Working with thoughts is difficult and demanding. Most patients run away from this exhausting stage. It is the main reason why depression does not go away. But if we are not willing to change the system of thinking that causes and maintains depression, it will always run after us and will always touch us with its shadow wing.

The ICAR procedure has four fundamental stages: Identification, Countering, Alternatives and Repetition.

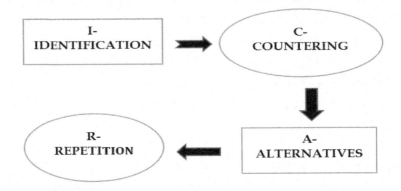

IDENTIFICATION (I)

In the first stage, the goal is to identify thoughts that sustain depression. We can do this by analyzing the inner language. What we are saying to ourselves when we are depressed?

Below are some examples of thoughts that may arise during difficult times: *"I have disappointed everyone. I am a weight on others shoulders. I'm guilty for everything that happens to me. Nobody really cares about me. I'm a total failure. Nobody needs me."*

Beneath is a list of the most common thoughts that occur when the mind becomes depressed. Use it with confidence and invest time in identifying specific problems in your thinking life. Complete the list according to other thoughts that do not give you peace.

Possible thoughts in depression [48]

1. I'm not good at anything.

2. Nobody cares about me.

3. I disappointed everyone.

4. I am a very weak man.

5. I am truly a burden to others.

6. I couldn't do anything.

7. I don't like myself.

8. My life is a great failure.

9. Nobody loves me.

10. The world is very bad.

11. Nothing makes sense anymore.

12. I am guilty of everything that happens.

COUNTERING (C)

The challenge and counteraction of thinking involve a change of attitude. [49] The events we went through may be painful and difficult to accept. But it is our duty to deal with what has happened to us. By counteracting bad thoughts, they lose their power. This process of countering is one of the most difficult things for someone who is tired and hit by the onslaught of thoughts. **However, we have to dare**. *There are several ways we can confront our thoughts:*

1. Counteracting at the behavioral level

It can be done using behavioral experiments or "Do the exact opposite of what depression tells you to do" technique.

Counteracting through behavioral experiment involves creating experiences through which we can test, directly, through facts, the thoughts that bother us. It is one of the most effective methods because by using it the mind learns much better than from various explanations. The technique involves choosing a thought and creating a situation through which we can directly test that thought, to see how true it is. Suppose one of the thoughts that surrounds you and what you believe in is, "*I am a burden to others.*

How do we proceed? We can make a list of 5 people around us and going to ask them if we are really a burden to them. You will be surprised when you realize how much your thoughts can differ from reality. Behavioral experiments are based on the thought you have identified. Find creative and suitable variants through which you can test the validity of your thoughts or what your mind invents.

Counteracting by technique Do the exact opposite of what your mind tells you

It is a useful strategy because it shows us we can initiate an action opposite to the thought from our mind. For example, if our thoughts tell us to flee into the desert and isolate ourselves from everyone, we do the exact opposite, deliberately seeking contact with others. If the thought tells us that nothing makes sense, we do something meaningful and valuable that makes sense. You can use both behavioral experiment strategies or do the exact oppposite of what your mind tells you, depending on the type of thoughts that upsets you.

2.Counteracting at the level of the mind

It is one of the most used and current tools for disputing thoughts in psychotherapy. The most common techniques for restructuring our thoughts are: *evidence analysis, logical analysis, pragmatic analysis, metaphors and narratives.* [50]

Evidence analysis

Suppose the thought that stops you from doing something to feel better is, *"Nothing makes me feel better."* Our task is to see if this thought is supported by evidence. Simply put, let's think about questioning this idea. Was there anything today and yesterday that made me feel better? Most of the time you will be surprised to find that there are such things.

Whether it's a tea you drank, a walk, or a person you've talked to. Use the questions to analyze the thought: Is there really nothing I do that makes me feel a little better? In this way, you will notice how the stability of the thought begins significantly to falter.

Logical analysis

It involves making a correction to the general conclusions that we have drawn from a particular event. There is a great possibility we are wrong when we come to conclusions such as: "*Life is a burden. God forgot about me, Nobody cares about me.*" When we come to such conclusions, we do so because we extract a general rule that is applied to a specific situation.

Use questions to examine thoughts and correct erroneous conclusions. For instance: Has life always been a burden? Is it logical to think that it is a burden just because I am going right now through a difficult situation? If God doesn't answer to me now, does it mean 100% that He forgot about my existence? Is there another alternative to this thought?

Pragmatic analysis

It is one of the strategies that patients prefer the most. This involves examining the usefulness of a thought. Suppose that the evil thought is this: "*I'm not good at anything, it makes absolutely no sense to do anything else.*"

The next step is to look at the impact this thought has on me. Does it really help me to think this way? When I think that I am nobody and nothing of what I do is irrelevant, how does it make me feel? What actions do I take when this thought comes to mind?

Metaphors and Narratives

When bad thoughts attack our minds, what we can do is to use the resources we have. We can, for example, read a suitable parable, listen to a testimony, read a story, watch a movie, read a psalm, or a verse that addresses the thoughts we have at that moment.

Reading a parable from the Bible, it can itself struggle with various contents of our mind. Because the Bible, the Word of God, is full of power. The thoughts, actions and whole life of Jesus are fascinating examples that change our minds. Our minds, understands and assimilates narratives much better. This is why Jesus largely used the parables.The central idea is that by studying certain narratives and metaphors that have power, we can change our world and with God's help we can substantially reduce the impact of depression.

ALTERNTIVES (A)

If we have managed to get rid of those difficult thoughts that keep us depressed, in order for this gain to be sustained, it is fundamental to formulate other thoughts to replace them. Another mental, healthy and undistorted content, a functional alternative. For example, if we think for a long time: *''Nothing makes me happy''* a healthy alternative to confronting thoughts may be: '' *There is still one thing or a few things I can do and make me feel happy."*

Maybe to have a tea or to go for a walk with my friends. I can read a chapter from the Gospel of Matthew. When you notice that thought tends to invade your mind again, remember it is a lie and tell it the true and functional version. Communicate this functional variant to him, until you see that thought has died out and is no longer dangerous for you.

REPETITION (R)

Even it's not true, most of the patients I worked with believe that if they win the battle at some point, with a certain thought, the problem has been solved. But this is a misconception. If you have repeated a thought that is false 1,000 times, it is impossible that by repeating the functional version 100 times, things will be completely resolved. It takes repetition and patience.

The truth is setting you free, but it must be pointed out every time when the lie tends to appear. If you tell yourself for 1,000 times that you are a loser who didn t achieve anything, but to compensate you will also state for 10 times that there were a few things you have done right, what do you think would have more impact upon you? Those 1,000 times of undistructive thoughts or those few positive statements?

The key is to resume the entire process until you reach the point where you are convinced that you have won the battle with that thought. An evil thought may occur in several situations. Repeat the whole process until you see that the truth has set you free.

Dare

I read few words and i want to share them with you: "*Bad thinking is any uncontrolled thought. Thoughts must serve us, not tyrannize us,*" Richard Wurmbrand. You may not be able to counteract certain thoughts. And this is normal. But don't give up. As the Apostle Paul teaches us, God has given us the ability to have care about our mind and to fight with negative thoughts. Bad thoughts means bad emotions.

At the end of this chapter, I want to remind you that a healthy thinking life leads to a healthy mind. Negative thoughts cause and maintain depression. It is important to remember that our thinking is the most vulnerable area of the mind. May God give you clarity to identify bad thoughts, counteracting them and consistently replacing them with healthy, true, and positive ones.

CHAPTER 10. Physical Activity

"A true athlete is a knight in all manifestations of life," Liviu Rebreanu.

Looking back on all the epochs before us, we can see that every day, people have carried out various movements and activities. Most of them had a significant impact on human physical and mental development. God Himself gave Adam and Eve free will in the Garden of Eden to engage in all kinds of physical activity.

If we make a brief comparison, we notice that in ancient times human life was very different from what it is today. The man had to run many kilometers to get food, climb, swim, jump. He fought various predators or sometimes simply ran out of their way. Nowadays, man no longer runs long walks to get food. He drives to work. He doesn't climb anymore, he climbs directly with the elevator where he needs to go. He is no longer on the move, being in the office chair most of the day.

The central idea is that although we no longer need to do so much exercise to survive, it has remained necessary for our minds and bodies to engage in physical activity every day.

Physical activity and health

In a study published in 2006, the Canadian Medical Association Journal summarizes about 50 years of research aimed to investigating the health benefits of physical activity. [5] Following this study, numerous indisputable evidences of the efficiency of regular physical activity were highlighted. Physical activity has had a significant impact on the prevention of many chronic diseases: cardiovascular disease, diabetes, obesity, hypertension, diabetes, depression, osteoporosis and premature death.

The central idea, derived from this research, is that the more regular physical activity people have, the better their long-term health. Evidence suggests there is a strong relationship between the level of physical activity and on how our health and body will look like.

People who have practiced physical activity showed a much lower risk between 20-35%, up to 50% of dying prematurely due to chronic diseases. More importantly, in cases where people were suffering from a chronic (cardiovascular) disease, physical activity is recommended because it is an effective strategy in preventing worsening health or premature death.

The main advantages of a physically active life are related to strengthening the heart muscles, slowing down the deterioration in old age, reducing heart rate and lowering blood pressure, reducing the mortality rate by about 50%. [52]

Physical activity and brain health

The fact that we stay physically active seems to play a huge role in maintaining brain health. Research in the field of neuroscience indicates that regular movement helps to increase certain substances involved in the development, repair and protection of nerve circuits.

One of these substances is BDNF (brain-derived neurotrophic factor) which is positively influenced by physical activities. In short, depression, anxiety and chronic stress contribute to the deterioration of neural networks, an aspect that is associated with many physical and somatic symptoms.

The substance BDNF, allows neurons to restore their neural processes. Moreover, BDNF contributes to the development of new neurons in the hippocampus, a key structure responsible for memory, learning and emotional regulation. [53]

Psychotropic drugs prescribed by a psychiatrist for anxiety and depression, act mainly on neurotransmitters to relieve the symptoms of depression. The fascinating aspect is that physical activity will do the same thing (releasing chemicals used by neurons to communicate with each other).

These neurotransmitters regulate the activity of the brain circuits that are involved in pleasure, reducing pain, inducing relaxation, reducing anxiety and depression. [54] When we take care of ourselves and move our body, the mind begins to release endorphins, serotonin and dopamine.

When we are physically active, the blood flow and oxygen in the brain improves, favoring the development of the brain. When we are disturbed, physical activity acts as a buffer against damage to the nerve networks, relaxation and recovery of the mind.

Those people who performed regular physical activity reported fewer symptoms of depression, anxiety and greater resistance to stress.

Also, the occurrence of anxiety and depression disorders among people who are physically active is much lower. [55] In a fascinating study that included 10,000 participants, people who performed daily activities had much fewer depressive symptoms.

The benefits have been maintained for the next 25 years. [56] In other words, there are many controlled clinical studies which show that regular exercise has a great effect in reducing the symptoms associated with depression and a medium effect in reducing the symptoms of anxiety.

This means that we have enough evidence about the clinical effectiveness of exercise, which can be compared to medication or psychotherapy. [57]

Exercising contributes to the development of the feeling of success. Thus, self-confidence increases the likelihood of continuing. [58]

How exactly do we proceed?

Small changes, made constantly, can bring benefits in reducing the symptoms of depression and maximizing physical and mental health. Keep in mind, you don't need to exaggerate with physical activities. In time you will discover those activities that suit best you and make sense to you.

A Chinese proverb says that one who moves a mountain begins by carrying small stones. Among the physical activities we can perform are general physical activities, recreational physical activities and high-intensity physical activities.

Choose the ones you like the most.

General physical activities

In this category we find simple and easy to implement activities. For example, walking to the store or a few stops to work, climbing stairs instead of using the elevator, doing various activities in the garden. This type of activity is recommended to be done daily for 30 minutes. The idea is to be done constantly and as often as possible.

Recreational activities

Such activities may involve various sports games such as tennis, basketball, volleyball, football, nature or fitness cycling, aerobics, stretching exercises. Running and swimming also fall in this category. The recommendation is to do it on average 2-3 times a week, 60 minutes each session.

Intense physical activities

It is recommended to be done from time to time. This pattern includes mountain climbing or participation in various marathons and competitions. Most of the activities mentioned are quite accessible. You can plan to walk 5,000 steps a day or climb different floors. Therefore, the goal is not for you to be a real athlete or to be a champion in climbing the floors. You don't even have to reconfigure yourself all the time. Physical and mental health is based on activities that are simple, useful and performed with moderate effect.

Start with small steps

Choose a specific day of the week when you can get a few steps in or an evening where you can walk for 30 minutes. Next week, do the exact same thing, but instead of doing it once a week, do it twice.

It is essential to choose physical activities that make sense to you. If running doesn't fascinate you in any way, don't bother with it. Instead, you can walk the dogs at a brisk pace for 30 minutes. The idea is for you to enjoy these activities. Whether it's aerobics and not swimming or running and not walking.

A particularly important aspect in this issue is consistency. Instead of striving to swim hard once a week, go for 30 minute daily walks. It takes a lot of perseverance and patience. There is definitely time in the day that you are wasting or waiting for TV commercials or watching mundane shows that don't please you. Get up from the couch and do some exercise. There is a better chance that you will be able to complete the activities if you plan them together with someone. Usually, the immediate costs are quite high: we get tired quickly, extra expenses can occur, but the positive effects are built over time and the results require patience.

Run in such a way that you receive the prize.

The Bible often compares service with running. Moreover, it urges us to take care of our body. Physical activity is one of the best medicines we can use against depression, anxiety and stress. If we are active and full of energy, the mind will begin to think and function as it was designed to do!

CHAPTER 11. Where Is God When We Suffer

"Genius can be formed in the quiet of a library, but strength of character is often the result of a life lived on the anvil of suffering," **Richard Wurmbrand.**

God's greatest people have raised the same question.

Looking at the greatest men of Scripture, we can see that they had this concern in their minds. The cruel reality they went through contributed to the belief that God was no longer among them. When what happens to us has nothing to do with what we do, we tend to believe that God is no longer in control of everything.

If we do good and receive evil, it is justified to have the impression that God no longer observes what is happening in the world. That He treats us unjust and unjustly. But we know that God often allows suffering to come in our life to give us the impetus we need to change.

Where is God when it hurts?

The answer is quite simple, but difficult to accept. Where it has always been. The truth is that God never changes His position. He is sovereign and always in control of all things. If we look at God's people, we can conclude some extremely important things.

First of all, God by His nature never disappoints. We may sometimes fail to accurately represent Him, but the Creator of Heaven and Earth does not fail. He never stopped to watch and to give us the strength to endure the difficulties of life. Moreover, when those around hurt our feelings and do not behave after our expectations, we tend to blame Him and attribute this to God. Basically, God is to blame for everything.

God did not disappoint his people in any way. He did not disappoint His people and did not disappoint any of those He loves. But just as in the case of Job, who did good and received evil, we are inclined to believe that God has left us helpless when things are difficult and don't work as we expect. Studying the Word of God, we can see that there is no man whom God has forsaken without reason. We are told in Genesis 8:1 that God remembered Noah and all the creatures that were in the ark. No matter how big the situation, God does not forget about us.

Negative emotions and perception of things

The truth is that we often think with emotions. If we feel betrayed and sad, our ability to put things together and see the truth and purpose behind the troubles is affected. It is therefore fundamental to take care of our mental and emotional health, because it is the only way we can have a correct and undistorted perspective on God.

Isn't it interesting that we ask ourselves questions about God's presence, mostly when it's hard for us? When we have intense negative emotions, what we have to do is to take care of our emotions and then we will be able to answer much more clearly and accurately the questions regarding the presence and existence of God.

Moreover, many of those who believed in God but now they stopped doing so, were people who were disappointed, concluding that God had forsaken them and no longer exists. All of this, often due to emotional pain and depression that

93

can creep into our minds. The moment we suffer, the mind no longer knows as clearly, at intuitive level, what is true and what isn't. Therefore, in this book you will find tips and exercises to help you balance your emotions and improve your mood.

Is Depression a sin?

If we want to answer this difficult question fairly, it is fundamental to look at things in depth. Is any disease a sin? Is cancer a sin? In some parameters, the answer may be yes, but not necessarily in all cases. Globally, obviously all diseases and illness have arisen because man has broken and overturned the rules established by God. When we live by ourselves and violate pre-established standards, we turn away from God and this can be considered a sin.

However, many of the mental disorders also have a genetic basis, therefore they were transmitted to us by our parents to a certain extent. The most important aspect, which I want to emphasize strongly is the following: no matter what illness and problem we have, it is our duty to trust God using all the resources and options He has left at our disposal. It is a sin to hurt yourself and your own mind, due to the fact that you blame yourself for sinning and so you have reached the end of your powers, tired in the fight against depression.

So, in this book you will find ways to fight with thoughts that cause you suffering and do not let you function at full capacity. Along with the information you have about depression, this material contains various validated tools to help you live a life much closer to what God intended for each one of us. I encourage you to test with confidence and practice with patience and forethought. Also, the notes from the references can be studied to expand the knowledge about these problems.

It is our duty to dare

The greatest satisfaction is when you learn to be patient and work with your own mind. There is a great joy, when you see that from a depressed and discouraged person, now you can enjoy the life you have, your family, friends and everything God has given you.

However, I would like to point out an extremely important issue at the end of this book. God always does His duty, but He will never do what we have to do. Do your best to do your part, and the results will improve as a consequence of prayer and the use of all the resources God has made available for us. I want to point out that this book does not fully address all of the issues that are related to depression and sadness. However, by applying these methods that have empirical support and are well studied, you will gain a much better chance of feeling better and being better.

Conclusion

We have reached the end of this journey and this is a very encouraging sign. I want to congratulate all of you who have shown patience and come this far, investing in the most precious thing: *your mind*. The fact that you have been patient so far is a good sign that you care and you are also concerned about how the mind works in various difficult circumstances.

I hope that after reading this material, you will be left with some stable ideas about what things we can do when we get tired and feel like there is nothing left for us. The purpose of this book was to address the issue of depression from two main perspectives: *the scientific one and the biblical one.*

After noticing that there are many people who trust in God but suffer in silence and there are few accredited resources about this suffering, I decided to address this issue.

Remember that you will not get very far if you are not involved and consistent with everything you do. Arm yourself with perseverance and results will start to show up.

Only you have the power to implement these truths in your daily life and build a stronger mind.

Finally, I hope this book has been helpful and I would be grateful if you will share it with your friends or give it to someone who is in dire need of it. Also, a sincere review will help me improve things in the future (here is the link where you can leave your honest review or you can insert this link manually into your browser https://amzn.to/3jWXf0P). May God give you much health and help you to guard your mind more than anything, because for out of it is the wellspring of life.

Bibliography

CHAPTER 1. The trap

[1] World Health Organization:WHO.

[2] General Statistics (USA) https://save.org/about-suicide/suicide-facts/

[3] Blazer, D. G. (2009, March 6). The depression epidemic. Christianity Today. Retrieved from https://www.christianitytoday.com/ct/2009/march/15.22.html

[4] You Can't "Pray Away" a Mental Health Condition

[5] New Testament, John 11:39.

[6] C.S. Lewis-Surprised by Joy, pg.102.

CHAPTER 2. The Biblie and Depression

[7] Holy Biblie New Living Translation.

[8] World English Biblie, King James.

CHAPTER 3. What is Depression

[9] I had a black dog, his name was depression (subtitrare în română).

[10] Diagnostic and Statistical Manual of Mental Disorders, 5th Edition: DSM 5.

[11] 5 Signs Of Depression That Should Never Be Ignored (youtube)

[12] https://www.webmd.com/depression/guide/depression-

complications#1

[13] Drevets, W. C., Price, J. L., & Furey, M. L. (2008). Brain structural and functional abnormalities in modd disorders:implications for neurocircuitry models of depression. Brain structurare and function, 213(1-2), 93-118.

[14] Caspi, A., Sugden, K., Moffitt, T. E., Taylor, A., Craig, I. W., Harrington, H., ... & Poulton, R. (2003). Influence of life stress on depression: moderation by a polymorphism in the 5-HTT gene. Science, 301(5631), 386-389.

[15] Depresia boala modernității. Dr Samuel Pfeifer.

[16] The vast majority of diseases do not have a single cause, they involve an accumulation of reasons. Formulated in simpler terms, a glass of water consists of many drops of water. Therefore, depression involves a combination of factors that interact with each other

CHAPTER 4. The causes of Depression

[17] https://www.webmd.com/depression/guide/causes-depression#1

[18] Goldman, N., Glei, D. A., Lin, Y. H., & Weinstein, M. (2010). The serotonin transporter polymorphism (5-HTTLPR): allelic variation and links with depressive symptoms. Depression and anxiety, 27(3), 260-269.

[19] Martin, B. (2020). What are the Risk Factors for Depression?. Psych Central. Retrieved on May 13, 2020, from https://psychcentral.com/lib/what-are-the-risk-factors-for-depression/

[20] Lewinsohn, P. M. (1974). A behavioral approach to depression.

Essential papers on depression, 150-172.

[21] Beck, A. T. (2008). The evolution of the cognitive model of depression and its neurobiological correlates. American Journal of Psychiatry, 165(8), 969-977.

[22] Beck, A. T., & Haigh, E. A. (2014). Advances in cognitive theory and therapy: The generic cognitive model. Annual review of clinical psychology, 10, 1-24.

[23] Winston Churchill about his depressions (Black Dogs) (English subtitles-youtube)

[24] https://positivepsychology.com/learned-helplessness-seligman-theory-depression-cure/

CHAPTER 5. Treatment of Depression

[25] The Schopenhauer Cure-Irving D. Yalom.

[26] https://www.nice.org.uk/guidance/cg90 ;
https://www.apa.org/depression-guideline/guideline.pdf

[27] Hollon, S. D., Thase, M. E., & Markowitz, J. C. (2002). Treatment and prevention of depression. Psychological Science in the public interest, 3(2), 39-77.

[28] Cipriani, A., Furukawa, T. A., Salanti, G., Geddes, J. R., Higgins, J. P., Churchill, R., ... & Tansella, M. (2009). Comparative efficacy and acceptability of 12 new-generation antidepressants: a multiple-treatments meta-analysis. The lancet, 373(9665), 746-758.
.

[29] Cuijpers, P., Hollon, S. D., van Straten, A., Bockting, C., Berking, M., & Andersson, G. (2013). Does cognitive behaviour therapy have an enduring effect that is superior to keeping patients on continuation pharmacotherapy? A meta-analysis. BMJ open, 3(4),

e002542.

30 Fournier, J. C., DeRubeis, R. J., Hollon, S. D., Dimidjian, S., Amsterdam, J. D., Shelton, R. C., & Fawcett, J. (2010). Antidepressant drug effects and depression severity: a patient-level meta-analysis. Jama, 303(1), 47-53.

31 Driessen, E., Hollon, S. D., Bockting, C. L., Cuijpers, P., & Turner, E. H. (2015). Does publication bias inflate the apparent efficacy of psychological treatment for major depressive disorder? A systematic review and meta-analysis of US National Institutes of Health-funded trials. PloS one, 10(9), e0137864.

CHAPTER 6. Behavioral activation

32 Treatment Plans and Interventions for Depression and Anxiety Disorders, Leahy 2017.

33 Lejuez, C. W., Hopko, D. R., Acierno, R., Daughters, S. B., & Pagoto, S. L. (2011). Ten year revision of the brief behavioral activation treatment for depression: revised treatment manual. Behavior modification, 35(2), 111-161.

34 Lambert, N. M., Fincham, F. D., & Stillman, T. F. (2012). Gratitude and depressive symptoms: The role of positive reframing and positive emotion. Cognition & Emotion, 26(4), 615-633.

CHAPTER 7. Positive Emotion

35 Fredrickson, B. L. (2001). The role of positive emotions in positive psychology: The broaden-and-build theory of positive emotions. American psychologist, 56(3), 218.

36 Quoidbach, J., Mikolajczak, M., & Gross, J. J. (2015). Positive interventions: An emotion regulation perspective. Psychological bulletin, 141(3), 655.

[37] When we take care of those who are sadder than us, our well-being automatically increases, we feel useful and fulfilled. Moreover, charity is not just a well-defined command, but one of our most feared antidotes to depression.

[38] Crocker, J., & Canevello, A. (2008). Creating and undermining social support in communal relationships: The role of compassionate and self-image goals. Journal of Personality and Social Psychology, 95, 555-575.

[39] How to stop worrying and start Living-Dale Carnegie.

CHAPTER 8. Maximizing sleep quality

[40] Harrison, Y., & Horne, J. A. (2000). The impact of sleep deprivation on decision making: a review. Journal of experimental psychology: Applied, 6(3), 236.

[41] https://www.webmd.com/sleep-disorders/features/10-results-sleep-loss

[42] Lopez, R., Barateau, L., Evangelista, E., & Dauvilliers, Y. (2017). Depression and hypersomnia: a complex association. Sleep medicine clinics, 12(3), 395-405.

[43] Geoffroy, P. A., Hoertel, N., Etain, B., Bellivier, F., Delorme, R., Limosin, F., & Peyre, H. (2018). Insomnia and hypersomnia in major depressive episode: prevalence, sociodemographic characteristics and psychiatric comorbidity in a population-based study. Journal of Affective Disorders, 226, 132-141.

[44] Treatment Plans and Interventions for Depression and Anxiety Disorders, Leahy 2017, Insomnia pg. 50.

[45] Stein, M. D., & Friedmann, P. D. (2006). Disturbed sleep and its relationship to alcohol use. Substance abuse, 26(1), 1-13.

CHAPTER 9. **Winning the battle with bad thoughts**

[46] https://www.youtube.com/watch?v=WRRdSm4ZjX4

[47] Beck, A. T. (1963). Thinking and depression: I. Idiosyncratic content and cognitive distortions. Archives of general psychiatry, 9(4), 324-333.

[48] Krull, E. (2018). Depression and Letting Go of Negative Thoughts. Psych Central. Retrieved on July 10, 2020, from https://psychcentral.com/lib/depression-and-letting-go-of-negative-thoughts/

[49] https://www.therapistaid.com/therapy-guide/cognitive-restructuring

[50] Young, J. E., Rygh, J. L., Weinberger, A. D., & Beck, A. T. (2014). Cognitive therapy for depression.

CHAPTER 10. **Physical Activity**
[50] Warburton, Nicol & Bredin (2006). Health benefits of physical activity: the evidence. Canadian Med Assoc J, 174, 801-809.

[51] Warburton, Nicol & Bredin (2006). Health benefits of physical activity: the evidence. Canadian Med Assoc J, 174, 801-809.

[52] Taylor et al. (2004). Exercise-based rehabilitation for patients with coronary heart disease: systematic review and meta-analysis of randomized clinical trials. American J of Med, 116, 682-692.

[53] Stephens, T. (1998). Physical activity and mental health in the United States and Canada: evidence from four popular surveys. Prev Med, 17, 35-37.

[54] Manger, T. A. & Motta, R. W. (2005). The impact of an exercise

program of posttraumatic stress
disorder,anxiety and depression. Int J Emerg Ment Healh, 7, 49-57.

[55] Steptoe, A. et al. (1996). Sports participation and emotional
wellbeing in adolescents. Lancet, 347, 1789-1792.

[56] Paffenbarger Jr, R. S., Kampert, J. B., Lee, I. M., Hyde, R. T.,
Leung, R. W., & Wing, A. L. (1994). Changes in
physical activity and other lifeway patterns influencing
longevity. *Medicine and science in sports and exercise*, 26(7), 857-865.

[57] Broocks, A. et al. (1998). Comparison of aerobic exercise,
clomioramine and placebo in the treatment of anic disorder. Am J
Psychiatry, 155, 603-609.
[58]

https://www.ted.com/talks/wendy_suzuki_the_brain_changing_benefits_of_exercise/up-next?language=en

Printed in Great Britain
by Amazon

38916598R00059